Do Not Fear

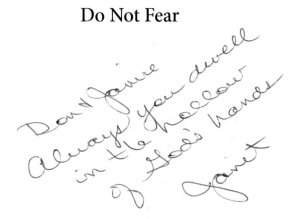

Don't fear
Always you dwell
in the hollow
of God's hands

Janet

Do Not Fear

Keeping the Faith in Troubled Times

Janet E. Hoover

WIPF *&* STOCK · Eugene, Oregon

DO NOT FEAR
Keeping the Faith in Troubled Times

Wipf & Stock
An Imprint of Wipf and Stock Publishers
199 W. 8th Ave., Suite 3
Eugene, OR 97401
www.wipfandstock.com

ISBN 13: 978-61097-956-6
Manufactured in the U.S.A.

For Ken whose support makes it all possible.

But now, thus says the Lord,
he who created you, O Jacob,
he who formed you, O Israel:
Do not fear, for I have redeemed you;
I have called you by name and you are mine.
When you pass through the waters,
   I will be with you;
And through the rivers, they shall not
   overwhelm you;
When you walk through fire you shall not be
burned,
And the flame shall not consume you.
For I am the Lord your God,
   the Holy One of Israel, your Savior.

—Isaiah 43:1–3a

Contents

Preface

FEAR IS a common human denominator. We are afraid of sickness and death. We are afraid of economic meltdown and terrorist attacks. We are afraid of looking ridiculous or of being lonely. We are afraid of disappointing others or ourselves. We want to be courageous and faithful, but sometimes feel overwhelmed by problems and struggles. Fear distorts and infects the lives of individuals, communities, and nations. As pervasive as fear is however, it is no match for the power and love of God. The antidote to fear is trust in God, but that trust does not always come naturally or in ten easy steps. One of the best ways to develop a trusting faith is to pay attention to the lives of men and women who themselves wrestled with fear and worry, individuals whose witness to faith weaves through the words of scripture. This book contains the stories of fifteen men and women who struggle with fear and who hear in the midst of their struggle: "Do not be afraid." Some of them are well known (Mary Magdalene, Peter, Moses); others are less familiar (Shiphrah, Malchus, Ananias). One of them (Pilate) ignores the call to courage. Each of these vignettes—based on scripture—offers glimpses into the hearts and minds of those whose encounters with God turned trembling into trust, doubt into hope, fear into faith.

Acknowledgments

THERE IS no way I can list all those individuals who have encouraged and supported, pushed and prodded me in my own journey from fear to strength. I have been blessed to have been part of five congregations where I was nurtured and challenged to become more than I ever imagined I could be: Westminster Presbyterian in Waterloo, Iowa where I was baptized and confirmed; St. Andrew Presbyterian in Iowa City, Iowa where I learned that Sunday School was not just for children and began a life-long love of religious education; Good Shepherd Presbyterian in Bartlesville, Oklahoma where I was encouraged and mentored to cast aside my fears and enter seminary; John Calvin Presbyterian in Tulsa, Oklahoma who welcomed and tolerated and accepted a fresh-from-seminary associate pastor; New Hartford Presbyterian in New Hartford, New York who had the courage to call a woman pastor from Oklahoma of all places and whose members witness to me on a daily basis, what it means to trust in a loving God. I have also been privileged to serve as chaplain with the New Hartford Fire Department where I have seen courage in action. Special thanks to George and Rosemary Moore whose faith in God worked its way into my heart and whose courage in dealing with life's challenges continues to inspire me. Finally, to Rachel, Katie, Jeremy, Kira, Alayna, and Sophia—I love you more than words can say.

1

Who's Afraid of the Big, Bad Wolf?

THE TWENTY-FIRST CENTURY began in fear—fear that life as we knew it would end as computer networks failed, bringing down our technological infrastructure. That particular anxiety proved groundless, but fear continues to weave its way through our days leaving in its wake depression, burnout, anxiety, violence, and despair. Strident terrorist threats, warnings of pandemics, cascading economic downturns, and whispers of scandal create a cacophony that beats in our ears until we want to add our own screams to the airwaves before hiding in some dark cave where we might find some peace and quiet.

We long to be brave and courageous and, like Superman or Wonder Woman, leap into the chaos and turmoil to help those in need and create order out of chaos. But the truth is, we are more like the three little pigs. In the children's story of three home-building pigs, heroism and strength dissolve in the face of impending danger. Sensing the presence of the big, bad wolf these three pigs scurried around in an effort to protect themselves. Two of them were so overcome with fear that they grabbed whatever they could find to shelter themselves. These pitiful shelters of straw and sticks, however, were no match for the snarling wolf, and as he huffed and puffed at their door, they were left exposed and vulnerable. Only one of the frightened creatures sought shelter in a structure strong enough to withstand the hot blast of the threatening, prowling wolf. Secure in a house of stone, only one little pig found the courage to face down the power of the wolf.

Who's afraid of the big, bad wolf? We are. We see him prowling on the horizon. We hear him growling at the door. We feel his hot breath on the back of our neck. We are afraid. We are afraid of sickness and death. We are afraid of looking ridiculous or being lonely. We are afraid of disappointing others or ourselves. We want to be courageous and strong, but our problems and struggles overwhelm us. The cold winds of broken dreams and dull routines, and the heated waves of quarrels and devastating illness combine to create a storm that beats against the walls we have erected in a vain effort to isolate ourselves from trouble. Our stockpile of self-protective resources—financial security blankets, educational credentials, and technological innovations—begins to crumble, leaving us bewildered and frightened.

When I was a child, one of summer's treats was to drive to the Amana Colonies where we would eat at the Ox-Yoke Inn. I looked forward to platters of chicken and bowls of corn and mashed potatoes, dishes of sauerkraut and cottage cheese with chives. But as we pulled into the parking lot, my stomach began to churn just a bit as fear began nudging my heart. The food was great, but upstairs, right next to the Ladies' Room where I couldn't avoid it, was . . . the bear. This was no ordinary stuffed bear. It was a monstrous creature with claws extended as if to inflict agonizing pain. An evil sneer contorted its face, and while I knew in my head it was long dead and could not hurt me, the rest of me was terrified. My heart would beat a little faster as I walked toward it, scurrying past as fast as I could. Years passed. Busy schedules and new responsibilities marked the end of this family tradition. Eventually, I moved from Iowa to Oklahoma and yet the bear never left my mind. For years it haunted my dreams.

Then one summer my husband and I took our daughters back to Iowa for a vacation and, hungry for some good Amana food, we bundled our daughters in the car and headed for the Ox-Yoke Inn. Along the way I prepared the girls for the bear so that they wouldn't be as frightened as I had been. I described the bear, stressing the fact that it was long since dead and totally harmless. And I prepared to face my fears. What a shock! I climbed the stairs and there was the same bear. The bear that had made my heart pound and caused sleepless nights well into adulthood was shorter than I, moth-eaten with a sickly sort of smile on its face.

My mind had built a monster out of a furry taxidermist-creation. My daughters continue to tease me about my scare bear, which helps remind me that sometimes the things we fear the most turn out to be nothing. The wolf howls fade into silence.

But not always. During the dark days of the Civil War in El Salvador, I had the experience of traveling to that broken and bleeding country where I met with many Salvadoran Christians. It didn't take long to grasp the fact that their faith was lived out in the midst of pain and fear. I heard stories of torture and killing and disappearances. I also heard—over and over again—testimonies of hope. One of these witnesses was a woman named Maria who shared the following:

> To be a Christian isn't easy. Oh, it is easy to read the Bible, go to meetings, receive communion. But at the same time we know that we and those we love will be persecuted, captured, and tortured for the cause of God. But we are to follow Christ and nobody is going to stop us. It is "yes" we have said to God. We do have fear—we are not courageous. We want to preserve our lives. Yet only God can take our life away. So we continue, despite our fear. I have had two children assassinated, but I have faith in God. All passes, but faith in God.

Sometimes the things we fear are all too real. We don't wake up from the nightmare. But the snarling wolves are not the final word, for in the end their growling is drowned out by melodies of grace and hope. Even as the wolf howls, a voice can be heard. Echoing out of the darkness it sings, "Be not afraid. I am with you always. Nothing can separate you from my love." Sometimes fear is as ephemeral as my Amana bear. Sometimes it is devastatingly real. But always and forever, God comes to us in the midst of our fear; breathing hope into all the dead and dried out places of our lives—energizing, encouraging, enlivening.

We will find ourselves in difficult situations, and in those times of trial and uncertainty, we have a choice. We can try to erect shelters of sticks and stones, hoping that a bigger pile of weapons or cash or accomplishments will protect us. But if we do, when it all crumbles around us— and it will—we will be left confused and vulnerable. Or we can find shelter in a structure built of living stones—men and women who allowed their faith to transform trembling into trust and doubt into hope. Living stones who witness to the truth that in Jesus Christ we need fear nothing. We can link hearts with those who know all too well the power fear has to inhibit loving trust and who know equally well the strength that is ours from a loving God. Some of these stones are well polished and highly visible—Moses, Esther, Peter, Mary Magdalene. Others are less obvious—Jacob, Jeremiah, Elizabeth, Joseph. Many of the stones are small and almost overlooked—Hagar, Shiphrah, Zebedee' wife, Malchus, Ananias, a nameless leper. Together, however, the stories of these living stones offer us hope for our own journeys of faith.

The wolf will come. We will face difficulties and pain and struggle. Suffering and hardship, trials and conflict come to all of us at one time or another. But they do not define us, as long as we allow ourselves to be shaped and formed by God's hands of grace and goodness. When anxiety mounts, when worries threaten to flatten our joy, when pain and darkness sweep us into the spiraling chaos, when we are afraid—we can remember the ways God has been present through the centuries to heal and restore. We can sing with Isaiah and all those who love God:

> Surely God is my salvation.
> I will trust, and will not be afraid,
> for the Lord God is my strength and my might;
> he has become my salvation.
>
> With joy you will draw water from the wells
> of salvation.

And you will say in that day:
Give thanks to the Lord,
call on his name;
make known his deeds among the nations;
proclaim that his name is exalted.

Sing praises to the Lord, for he has done gloriously;
let this be known in all the earth.
Shout aloud and sing for joy, O royal Zion,
for great in your midst is the Holy One of Israel.

—Isaiah 12:2–6

2

Streams in the Desert: Hagar

Genesis 16:1–16, 21:1–21

THE HOT wind etched an arid trail across the desolate landscape; a trail duplicated in Hagar's heart. "How," Hagar whispered with hardened lips and swollen tongue, "how is it possible to be so dry and yet cry so much?" Her swollen eyes, reddened by the relentless, burning sun, shifted toward her son. He was so still—eyes open but staring off into the distance as if he had already moved away from her. Her arms ached to hold him, but he was no longer an infant to be embraced. She slowly pulled her scarf from her head, stretching it over her son in an attempt to provide some sort of shade. Crawling away she almost welcomed the blistering heat on her head, as the pain served to distract her from her grief—a mix of sadness and anger that threatened to sweep her up into madness. In a life well salted by tears, this moment was beyond anything she had yet experienced. Crumpling into a heap of misery, her mind went back—back to her life before the great sadness.

It seemed unreal, those early years. Years when she was actually happy. Time and hardship had eroded the memories, but there were still a few images that she kept tucked away to pull out when reality became too hard to bear. She could still see her father's hands carving small animals out of pieces of wood. She remembered her mother's arms holding her and her mother's voice crooning a gentle lullaby. She remembered running and playing with her brother around the campfire.

The problem with memories is that once they started, they wouldn't stop. She wanted to stay in her mother's lap forever, but even now she could hear her mother's screams and feel the rough hands of the man pulling her away. She remembered her father lying motionless on the ground with her brother crumpled on top of him. She remembered feeling lost and alone in a land she didn't know, and the relief she felt when a sparkling-eyed woman—Sarah they called her—took her by the hand and said, "Child, you now belong to us. Soon you will be a nursemaid for my baby."

Slavery was a burden to be born, but at first she was grateful that as far as slavery went, her lot was not so bad. Sarah had been a fair and kind mistress—at least for a while. But as the months and years passed and the baby of whom Sarah had spoken never materialized, Hagar became a target for Sarah's grief and anger. Hagar tried to do her work as invisibly as she could, but she often found herself on the receiving end of Sarah's increasingly sharp tongue.

One day, Sarah hunted Hagar out as she was preparing the evening meal. As she spoke, her face tightened with a sort of desperate rage. "Leave it," she snapped. "Go wash yourself and come with me. Hurry girl."

Hagar splashed some water on her face, ran her fingers through her hair, and hurried to her mistress. As she approached, Sarah grabbed her by the arm and pulled her through the dusty camp straight to Abraham's tent. "Go in," she ordered. "He's waiting for you. Just do what you're told and don't ask questions."

The next hours were a blur of harsh color and sounds of panting and her own screams muffled by Abraham's calloused hand covering her mouth. By the time it was over, the sun had set and Hagar moved through the blessed darkness before finally crawling into her tent where tears of humiliation and pain soaked the shawl on which she pillowed her head.

She heard the whispers the next day; saw the other slaves looking at her with a mix of pity and disgust. The worst thing was the look on Sarah's face whenever Hagar crossed her path—loathing, eagerness, and grief all woven together. Abraham tried to be kind, but it was obvious her presence embarrassed him. For the next few weeks, Hagar did her work and then crept into her tent, curled up into a ball, and tried to disappear. Then one day, as Hagar walked past Sarah, Sarah's wrinkled hand reached out and grabbed her. Sarah's fingernails dug into Hagar's tender skin.

"Are you pregnant?" she demanded. Hagar bowed her head and nodded, tensing for the blow she expected. To her surprise she heard a harsh barking sound. She looked up and realized that Sarah was actually laughing. "This will have to do," Sarah muttered.

She must have said something to Abraham, because the next day Hagar was moved to a larger tent closer to the well. His awkward kindnesses soothed her soul, and she began holding her head high. "You'll be sorry," the other slaves muttered. "You may be pregnant, but you are just a birthing machine. You'll see."

And sure enough one day Sarah told Hagar to fetch her a cool cloth. Hagar began, "Ask someone else. I'm tired and after all, I am carrying Abraham's. . . ." Before she could finish the sentence, Sarah lashed out with fists and tongue, screaming and striking out with whatever she could get her hands on. Hagar did the only thing she could think of—she fled. She didn't get far, however, before she began gasping for breath. Finally, she collapsed on the ground, wrapping her hands around her swollen belly and waiting for . . . exactly what she wasn't sure. Maybe for Abraham to come looking for her and carry her back to camp. Maybe for Sarah to apologize. Maybe for some of her fellow slaves to talk her into returning. Maybe for a swift punishment that would put her out of her misery. But nothing happened as she lay in the dust for what seemed like hours, until at last her eyes closed and she slept.

It was in that place between sleeping and waking that she heard it. A voice that seemed to come from above her and within her at the same time. A gentle voice that caressed her spirit. An insistent voice that stirred her soul.

"Hagar," the voice said. "Running away is not the answer. Go back. Your job will not be easy. You will struggle, but you are not alone. Do not be afraid."

Hagar slowly opened her tear-swollen eyes expecting to see some sort of glorious light or god-like human being, but the only sign of life was a bird circling overhead. Even though the dryness of the landscape had not changed however, she felt a new strength coursing through her bones that lifted her to her feet and sent her moving back to Sarah.

Sarah had either not missed her, or knew that she had gone too far, for she never mentioned Hagar's absence. And so the weeks passed with Hagar quietly doing her tasks. The day her son, Ishmael, was born she had been surprised by the wave of love that coursed through her as she heard his first cry. Then, even before she had counted his tiny fingers and toes, Sarah had come and pulled Ishmael from her arms. It was heart-breaking—feeding him and then passing him back to Sarah; but as a slave Hagar knew better than to expect any long-lasting joy.

At first she thought maybe everything would be all right. She saw her son often and found little ways to show her love—a treat of dates and honey slipped to him as he played, a special way of squeezing his shoulder when they passed on the path. She loved watching Ishmael follow his father through the camp—imitating Abraham's walk, tilting his head just like Abraham when he was puzzled. And there were those times when mother and son sat together around the campfire and talked—Hagar sharing memories of the land and people who had given her birth. Every chance she had she sang to him. She took all her love and created a melody from her very soul: "Child of my heart, even if we part, I'll always love you, child of my heart."

As the flames of the fire died away, her voice would fade and the darkness would wrap itself around them, and even though it was Sarah who wrapped him up and carried him to bed, Hagar clung to a shadow of contentment.

Then everything changed. It seemed like a cruel joke at first. Sarah pregnant? But Hagar didn't laugh. A sickness began to move through her, a fear for her son and his future. She prayed that it was only a rumor. She prayed that Sarah would miscarry. She prayed that the baby would be a girl. But when Sarah delivered a healthy boy, Hagar began to be afraid. Initially, all seemed good—Ishmael was a wonderful big brother, guarding baby Isaac from any and all dangers. As Isaac grew, Ishmael was always there to patiently hold his hands and steady his tottery steps, to teach and encourage him with quiet words and gentle laughter. But one day, as Ishmael chased him in an exuberant game of tag, Isaac fell. As Ishmael bent to pick him up, Sarah came around the corner and saw her baby screaming. Swooping him up in her arms, she glared at Ishmael before she turned and marched toward Abraham's tent.

Cold, clammy fear gripped Hagar's heart as she watched Abraham walk towards her, his eyes shifting to the left and the right, and she knew. Wordlessly he handed her a bundle—a robe for Ishmael, a skin of water, some meal. That was it. No hug for his son. No look of regret for his son's mother. He just turned and shuffled back toward his tent. Ishmael's confusion was like a knife to Hagar's heart. "Daddy!" he screamed. But Abraham just kept moving. Hagar and Ishmael stood frozen in place as the tent flap was pulled back. Sarah stood for a moment silhouetted against the sky, her hand at her throat. Then slowly and deliberately she pointed toward the horizon and said simply, "Out."

That was it. Out. And then the tent flap fell. Hagar shifted the bundle to her head and turned—too worn out and afraid to cry. Ishmael followed her, pausing after every couple of steps to turn and stare at the tent, as if willing Abraham to come and call him back. But there was no sound. No movement. And so they left, the slightly stooped woman and the young boy, lips quivering as he fought back his tears.

They walked until it grew too dark to see and then sank to the ground for a few hours of what passed for sleep. Rising with the sun, they walked some more. And so it went—hour after hour, day after day. At last Hagar knew they could go no further. There was no more food, no water. The heat had leached away the last reserves of their energy. Dragging Ishmael by the hand she lurched to the only shady place she could see—a couple of scrawny bushes. She settled Ishmael under the larger of the two and tried to comfort him, singing, "Child of my heart . . ." But before she could finish, her voice cracked and anguish racked her spirit. Crawling away, she hid her face in her lap and wept.

At first she thought it was the wind whispering over the rocks, but then she began to distinguish words. "Hagar," the voice called. "Hagar, don't be afraid. I see you. You are child of my heart. I love you. You are not alone. Go hold your future."

With a sudden burst of energy she pulled herself to her feet and stumbled over rocks and thorns to cradle her boy. He was so still she wasn't sure if he was dead or alive. She just held him tight and rocked him, pouring all her love into his frail body, bathing him with her tears, and singing, "Child of my heart. I'll always love you. Child of my heart."

"Hagar," the voice whispered again. "Look and see my love."

She turned her head and there, just behind a rock, she saw the glint of sunlight off water. Water! Filling her water skin she pressed it to Ishmael's cracked lips, gently moistening them. After what seemed like hours, his head shifted, his lips parted, and he drank. With each swallow Hagar felt her own strength renewing. At last she understood. She understood that the future was not empty but filled with opportunities for her and for her son. There would be struggle and pain; she knew that. But God had seen her. God knew her name. She was not a piece of property, but a person. And as she and Ishmael set off, she hummed, "Child of my heart . . ."

3

Wrestling in the Dark: Jacob

Genesis 27:1—28:22, 32:1–32

JACOB WAS tired of running. Running from responsibility. Running from his brother's anger. Running for his life. Running from his life. Running from difficult, uncomfortable situations. Running to someplace—anyplace—where he could be safe. Sometimes he just wanted to stop, to rest. But whenever he slowed down, the hot breath of fear quickly drove him back on the run.

It used to be fun—playing with people's minds and managing situations so that he would come out on top. He had learned early that his easy way with words and his innocent-looking face got him out of all sorts of trouble. He could utter the most bold-faced lie with a look of such sincerity that no one saw through him to discover his incorrigible sneakiness and deceit. As a young man, he loved pushing the limits, seeing how far he could go before someone drew a halt to his machinations. It was especially fun manipulating his twin brother, Esau. Jacob began walking while Esau was still crawling in the dust, and one of his favorite games had been to run circles around Esau, who would finally sprawl flat, weeping in frustration at his inability to keep up with Jacob. Over and over he played the same tricks on Esau, and over and over Esau fell for them. Once in a while Esau's anger would boil over, but Jacob learned to recognize in Esau's clenched jaw and reddening brow, the volcanic fury about to erupt, and he would take off running. Confident that Esau would tire quickly, Jacob would head for a shady spot just out of sight of the camp where he would wait until he was sure that Esau's rage had quieted.

Then one day Jacob went too far. Usually the stakes of his trickery were small—an extra portion of figs, words of praise from his mother, fewer chores. This time, however, he stole the family birthright and blessing. Covered in a sheepskin so that he would smell like his brother after a day with the flocks, he disguised his voice and lied to his father. And he succeeded. This time, however, that success didn't sit well in his soul. When Esau discovered what Jacob had done, his roar of rage echoed through the family camp. That, however, wasn't what set Jacob running. It was the look on his father's face when he realized what Jacob had done. The shame and grief, the anguished horror reflected back on Jacob from Isaac's rheumy eyes, drove a spike of pain deep into Jacob's heart. Isaac's guttural, "No! No!" sent Jacob reeling.

Grabbing a cloak from beside his bed and sweeping up the bag in which his brother carried his lunch when he tended the flock, Jacob took off running as fast as he could. He ran until his legs trembled and his heart pounded, finally collapsing between two rocks where he pulled the cloak over his exhausted body. As he did, the scent of home—stew simmering over a wood fire, his mother's perfume and his father's hair oil—all of it wrapped around him and he wept for the beauty and the pain of all he had left behind. At some point, his breathing quieted and he fell into a fitful sleep. He dreamed of home—his brother's scream of anger, his mother's head bowed in grief, and his father's eyes, piercing and penetrating his soul. And then he saw a ladder stretching up into the star-spangled sky, reaching up past the clouds and the moon into the inky darkness. As he stared, the ladder burst into life with what looked like thousands of glowing lights, dancing up and down the rungs. The air was filled with the rustling of wings and music so alive and harmonic that he felt his heart break with the beauty of it.

Then he felt something brush across his cheek—a gentle stroke that whispered of grace and goodness. Even as he gasped with the joy of it, everything hushed. The lights faded and Jacob opened his eyes to see only rocks, and dirt, and a lizard scurrying away. But the dream was enough to still his fear, to lift him to his feet singing, "Surely God is here. Here in this place."

This moment of grace helped, but it didn't change the situation. Jacob's fear—fear of Esau's anger, fear of Isaac's disappointment, fear of his mother's pain—kept him on the run. But he continued with a courage born of hope, and the memory of God's song in his heart. The broken places in his heart still ached, but now the pain was bearable. Running away from his past into an uncertain future, Jacob held his head high for he knew that despite it all, God was with him.

The problem with holy moments, Jacob reflected later, is that they don't last. The glow of that moment was soon extinguished by hard work and the relentless routine of making a living. The years of his exile from home were not easy. He worked hard. Sometimes he laughed bitterly as he sheared the sheep or tramped through the lonely wilderness looking for a stray lamb, at the irony of it all. He had tried so hard to avoid this sort of work. He had cheated and lied and shattered his family in an effort to gain a reward without the labor. He ran from his guilt and his regrets only to end up doing what he should have done in the first place. Whenever these thoughts worked their way into his mind, he would head out of camp and run—as hard and as fast as he could. He would run as long as it took to drive the demons away. Then he would limp back to camp—exhausted but feeling somehow cleansed of sin and suffering.

As the years went by, his homesickness eased a bit. With a difficult and demanding father-in-law, four women to care for, ten sons, and a daughter, he didn't have time for much thinking. It was only when his beloved wife, Rachel, bore him a son that things changed. He looked into baby Joseph's eyes and saw not only the future, but also glimpses of the past; and he knew. He knew it was time to reconnect with his heritage, to transplant his family into the soil that had nurtured and shaped him. It was time to go home.

Preparations for going home took a while. Jacob had to gather flocks and provisions for the journey. He needed to instruct his wives in the ways of the new culture in which they would live and raise their children. He began telling his sons the family stories—tales of people they had never met and a God they didn't know. He talked about many things, but whenever one of his sons asked him why he had left that land, why he had turned away from his parents—Jacob grew silent. Eventually all was ready for the journey, but still Jacob delayed, finding one excuse after another to put off the trip for another day, another week. Finally Leah, his first wife, could take it no longer. She gathered water and then waited for Jacob to emerge from his tent. Striding toward him, she announced, "If we are going, then let's go. We can't live like this . . . packing, unpacking, repacking. If this is what you need us to do, then let's go today. Now."

Jacob stared into the wilderness and at last he whispered, "So be it." At that, everyone sprang into action, and within a matter of hours good-byes were shared and Jacob and his family headed back to the place Jacob longed for and feared at the same time. He had left home running. This time the pace was slower, for the closer they got, the greater Jacob's fear. Would Esau attack as soon as he saw them? Would his father denounce him and refuse him entry? Was his father even alive? One good thing about walking through the wilderness is that it gives a man time to think. At last Jacob figured out his strategy. He gathered a group of faithful slaves and sent them on ahead. "Tell Esau," he stammered, "Tell my brother that I am coming. Let him know that I return as a success."

As he watched the men head out, Jacob's fear threatened to choke him. Would Esau hear his message and be intimidated? Would he be jealous? Would he understand that Jacob would give him all his flocks and slaves if Esau would let his family live? All he could do now was watch and wait.

In hopes that if Esau attacked at least some of them might survive, Jacob divided the company into two groups. And then he did the only other thing he could think of to do. He prayed a prayer skillfully crafted to impress God with his sincerity. A prayer designed to remind God of the promises God had made. And just in case God wouldn't keep the promise, Jacob sent a gift ahead to appease Esau. Then he gathered his family and crossed the river, the final boundary between his two lives, the final boundary between safety and the uncertain future.

As the shadows darkened, Jacob sent everyone away before he lay down by the river. This time there was no starry sky, no glowing lights and angel choruses. Jacob tossed and turned as the darkness closed in. Suddenly, out of the silence, a shadowy figure leapt at Joseph. Too frightened to make a sound, Jacob did the only thing he knew how to do when attacked. He fought back.

Using every ounce of strength and cunning he could find, Jacob wrestled for his life. Hour after hour, through that long, dreadful night, Jacob looked for his opponent's weak spots, straining for any possible advantage. Heart pounding, Jacob made one last, desperate lunge for the stranger's throat. But even as his hands closed around his neck, Jacob felt a touch in the hollow of his thigh—a light touch and yet the pain coursed through his body. In that instant of blinding, debilitating torment, Jacob knew that his defeat had never been in question. Jacob's hands fell from the stranger's neck and he wrapped his arms around the man, clinging to him with a desperate longing. "Bless me," he cried. Even as his words echoed from the hills, he felt the pain ease and his fear faded away.

"Bless me," Jacob pleaded. As the sun rose, Jacob saw clearly for the first time in his life. He knew that the blessing he had craved ever since he was a young boy, was not to be obtained by wily intelligence or hard work. It was a sheer and glorious gift. Jacob dared to lift his head and as he looked up he saw a face strangely beautiful and at the same time as familiar as his own. A face that looked at him with eyes that seemed to pierce his soul; that saw every broken and rotting corner of his life, every doubt and fear. Eyes so filled with love and compassion that Jacob had to turn his head or be blinded by the light.

Jacob knew that his fears had been pinned to the mat, overpowered by mercy and love greater than any rebellion or betrayal. Jacob had been wrestled to the ground, and yet he felt as if somehow he had won the greatest victory of his life. He might limp into the future, but with each faltering step, he would be sustained by the greatness of God who loved even a sinner such as he.

4

The Courage to Care: Shiphrah

Exodus 1:8–21

SHIPHRAH OFTEN wondered why it was, with twenty-four hours a day in which to be born, so many babies entered the world by torchlight. Being a midwife meant sleepless nights and long hours spent encouraging pain-wearied women. Birthing in the heat of the day was unpleasant, but the shadowy darkness added an element of danger to the process, as it was easy to miss a woman's pallor or the blueish skin of a baby in distress. There were times, as she trudged home just as the sun peeked over the horizon, that she was tempted to give it all up—the late night calls for help, the frightened gasping sound of a woman in the last stages of the birthing process. The work was messy and challenging—especially when a nervous father or con-cerned grandmother settled under foot. Those frustrations, however, vanished after a good night's sleep. But there were certain births that haunted her dreams and ate away at her joy. Those times when her skills let her down or when her best efforts weren't good enough, times when babies came too early or with defects that made life impossible for them. Mothers died. Fathers turned their backs on daughters simply because they were not sons.

Things had gotten easier since Puah joined her in the work. Two midwives meant that night duty could be alternated. Two midwives meant occasional days off. But more importantly, now there was someone with whom to talk through the difficult cases. Four hands were better than two when mother and baby both went into distress.

Then one night it all fell apart. She could still hear the hammering on the door—not the frantic hurry-up rhythm of a frightened father, not the tentative rapping of a worried woman. This was different—a strong, authoritative, insistent pounding. The stony faces of the soldiers who stood there sent a chill up her spine. "Pharaoh wants you. Now!" one of them barked. Then, without waiting for her questions or listening to her pleas for time to pull herself together, they strode off into the darkness leaving her to hurry after them as best she could.

An audience with the Pharaoh was frightening in the best of times. Everything—ornate furnishings, larger-than life wall carvings, and armed guards—designed to intimidate and overwhelm visitors with majesty and power. Even now, in the middle of the night, the torches lining the room revealed huge marble statues, the sight of which made Shiphrah's skin crawl. Rising out of the shadows, Pharaoh looked somehow more than human. It was only as she looked at his hands that she caught a glimpse of a man under the trappings of divinity. Nails bitten to the quick, they trembled ever so slightly. His voice, however betrayed none of this—high-pitched and harsh it reverberated off the walls. "No more," he screamed. "No more Hebrew babies, do you understand. If you value your job, if you value your life, see to it that not one more Hebrew boy is born alive. Do whatever you have to, but no more babies!"

Shiphrah looked around waiting for someone to calm him, to escort him back to his room. Surely his mind was deranged. No more boy babies born alive? If he meant what she thought he meant . . . well, only a monster would kill babies. But, no one in the room even blinked. Then, he was gone. The room emptied, leaving Shiphrah alone. Stumbling out of the palace she wanted to cry or scream, anything to drown out the sound of that voice screeching, "No more babies!"

Shiphrah was truly and deeply afraid. If she ignored the Pharaoh's command, her life was at risk. She would not only lose her freedom to work, she would surely lose her life. But if she obeyed? Her brain would not let her go that direction. To kill simply because Pharaoh was afraid was an affront to God. The choice was terrible: Pharaoh or God? Death or life?

She prayed for clarity. She prayed for wisdom. She prayed for Pharaoh to change his mind in the clear light of day. But she didn't have the luxury of time. As she turned down the alley leading to her room, one of the Hebrew slaves grabbed her arm. "I've been looking everywhere for you," he gasped. "It's time, praise God. My wife is about to deliver. She is asking for you. Please hurry."

Shiphrah's heart began pounding in her chest and even as she hurried along, she began rehearsing what she might say: "These things just happen. He was simply too weak. The cord was around his neck." As she neared the slave hut, she was relieved to see Puah crouched outside the door, preparing the birthing instruments. She paused only to whisper to her, "Just do what I tell you. I'll explain later." Then, throwing off her cloak she hurried to the slave woman's side.

"Please leave," she ordered those gathered around the mother's bed. "She needs quiet." Despite the turmoil in her head and heart, she began working instinctively, going through the motions of her job without conscious thought. As births go, this one was quick—too quick as far as she was concerned. As the head crowned, she choked out the only prayer she could manage, "God, help me." Even as she muttered these words, the mother pushed and Shiphrah caught a perfect little boy. He opened his mouth and her hand hovered—ready to choke that first breath from his body. She looked into his eyes and knew what she had to do. Wrapping him tightly she muffled his cries with her body, urgently whispering a warning to his mother, before placing the gently breathing baby in her arms.

God help her, there was now no going back. She was afraid, but fear of Pharaoh was less important than the fear of living with shame and guilt. Once again, she was thankful for Puah's presence, for this gut-wrenching decision was easier now that there were two to deal with the consequences. From that moment on, she and Puah worked together—one of them handling the birth and the other masking the lusty cries of the newborns. Before Pharaoh's edict when someone asked her why on earth she did what she did, her immediate reply was, "The joy of hearing a baby's first cry. That makes it all worth while." Every time she heard the cry her heart had smiled, for there—wrapped up in flesh and bone—was hope and promise, love and joy. Now that cry was a sound to be dreaded, for it might alert the soldiers to the fact that there were more babies. Once mothers smiled as they heard their new babies announce their arrival with outraged cries. Now they learned tricks to silence even the slightest whimper lest Pharaoh's minions overhear.

Weeks and months passed during which tiny babies became active toddlers—too big to hide. Mothers struggled to find ways to keep these children safe and away from Pharaoh's attention. Shiphrah even heard of one mother who found a way to save her child by arranging circumstances so that Pharaoh's daughter herself stepped in to save the child. Shiphrah wished she could remember that particular woman, that particular baby, but she had learned to see only what she had to, lest she be forced to betray the lives she had worked so hard to bring into the world.

And then it came again, the knock in the night. This time both women were hustled through the dark streets straight to Pharaoh's throne room. The soldier at the door grabbed Shiphrah by the arm and threw her across the floor toward Pharaoh's feet.

"I told you," he screamed. "I told you no more Hebrew babies."

"Yes sir," Shiphrah murmured, assuming these would be her last words. "We try our best, but they are a strong and persistent people, and before we even get there, their children are born and out of sight. After all, we are just two women." Then she waited. The silence grew and grew until it seemed as if it would drown her. At last she dared to lift her head. Pharaoh sat there, head in his trembling hands.

Slowly she stood, grabbing Puah by the hand. Carefully one inch at a time, she backed out of the room, the only sound the shuffling of bare feet on the stone floor. The last thing she saw before she turned to run for home was Pharaoh looking at her with empty eyes.

For a long time, Shiphrah and Puah kept this night to themselves. But as the years passed and they had their own children, they spoke of it more often. "Fear is a funny thing," Shiphrah would say. "Frightening moments come, times when your decision to act or not act, love or ignore, reach out or turn away, will affect your whole life. Do not let fear blind you to the power of love. Have the courage to care, and when you do, that which is born may be more freeing than anything you can imagine."

5

On Holy Ground: Moses

Exodus 2:1—4:20

IT NEVER failed. Every time Moses sat down before a camp-fire, he remembered—a remembering that warmed his heart as well as his hands and feet. Moses never forgot that day—the day his fear was burned away. Years had passed. Years of great joy and great sadness. Years of mountaintop adventures and anguished loneliness. But that one moment never left his mind. It was as if he himself had been cast into a fire where all his guilt and insecurity and doubt had been burned away, leaving him clean and new and strong. For years he held the moment in his heart, preferring to mull it over in silence, hesitating to share something that could not be explained rationally, afraid that he would be laughed at or mocked as a foolish old man. But as time went by, he knew he needed to share what he had seen and heard.

Leading his people was more than charting a course through the wilderness, more than providing food and medicine, more than shaping disparate individuals into a community with laws and rituals. Leading meant telling his story. Sharing his story might lodge his memory among a people who, in the years to come would need to remember where they came from and whose they were. More than once he struggled to put the indescribable into words, to put the glory of God into nouns and verbs. He wished Aaron were still alive, for Aaron was the articulate one. But Aaron was long dead and so Moses dug deep into his soul, praying that God would once more come to his rescue. One night as the fire crackled and the light of the flames danced in the eyes of those huddled around it, he knew that the time had come, and so he cleared his throat and began:

Midian was a place of blessing, a sanctuary when I needed it most. I found work and family and safety among its people. I was content. And yet sometimes, when the sun beat down or I caught a smell of bread baking, I felt an ache inside of me, a longing for the streets of Egypt—the land of my birth. Homesickness washed over me and I would weep for all that was missing from my life. It wasn't the pomp and circumstance of life in the palace that I wanted, it was simple things—the sound of traders bartering their goods, my mother's smile, the games I played with the other boys, the taste of honey drizzled over a plate of dates. Egypt was in my bones—her smells and sounds defined my days. Growing up I lived and breathed Egyptian air, yet even as a young boy I knew there was something about me that was different—something other than my royal status. In the beginning I asked my mother why I felt that way, but each time it was as if a veil fell across her eyes and while her words were meant to reassure me, the tone of her voice told me that I was entering into a place of danger. So I learned to avoid the questions. When the strangeness descended upon me, I shrugged it off. I knew that I was loved and that was all that mattered.

But these feelings of doubt and uneasiness never really left me. As I grew up I began to notice things that everyone else around me took for granted, but made me uncomfortable. It became harder for me to enjoy my meals when those who served me trembled with hunger. I cringed every time a palace official snapped at one of the servants. I felt some sort of bond with these Hebrew slaves, and as I watched them work hard and struggle with illness and the brutality of the overseers, anger on their behalf rose up in me.

One day, as I watched one of the guards beating a Hebrew slave because he hadn't moved fast enough, my anger erupted and the next thing I knew the guard was dead. Even though I was a prince of Egypt, I had crossed the line. I knew I had only one choice—to flee for my life. I raced home, brushing my slaves aside, pulling the curtain to my sleeping quarters shut. Tears stung my eyes and my hands trembled as I pulled the blanket from my bed and began throwing my possessions into it. I heard muffled conversation from the other side of the curtain, but was too busy to listen. Suddenly the curtain parted and two slaves—a young man and woman appeared. I yelled at them to go away, but they planted themselves on either side of me and while I stood immobilized they told me a story. They said that they were my brother and sister, and they offered me a blessing for my journey. Imagine the pain and confusion tumbling around my head and my heart: guilt over my deed of violence, the shock that comes from discovering that I was not of royal stock as I had always believed, anguish at the thought of being exiled from the land I knew as home. I heard what they said, but their voices seemed to come from a place far away. Even as they were still talking, I brushed them aside and left. I left the woman who had raised me and loved me. I left a life of privilege and power. I couldn't bear to look back, running and running until I could run no more, propelled by an unvoiced scream. Eventually I found a home in Midian and there I licked my wounds and put the pieces of my life back together. I found a wife and work as a shepherd. All was well until that day in the desert.

I was simply going about my business, preoccupied with a small lamb that appeared to be limping and the ewe whose breathing didn't sound quite right. My main concern was getting the flock back to my father-in-law without losing even one of the sheep entrusted to my care. I wasn't thinking about anything except the fact that my feet hurt. Scanning the horizon I looked for a spot to sit and rest for a bit. That was all I wanted.

I knew the minute I saw the dancing flames that something profound was happening. As a young man I had participated in many Egyptian religious ceremonies in temples and palaces. I had watched the procession of priests moving into the courtyard, led by a priest carrying a flaming torch—sign of the presence of the god whose day we celebrated. I had watched the flame carried to the highest point of the palace where the priest announced, "The great god Amon is now here in this place." Or maybe, "The great goddess Isis is now here in this place." The understanding engrained in me from the time I was old enough to walk was the importance of the flaming torch. As long as the flame burned, that particular god or goddess was present within the walls that surrounded us.

So when I saw the flames I moved closer. As I did, everything changed. I heard a voice—not some priest announcing God's presence, but a voice alive with cadences of power and might, a voice calling me by name. The flames told me that I was standing in a place of holiness, but instead of a beautiful temple erected by human hands, creation itself was imbued with glory and majesty. As my heart pounded and knees trembled, a feeling of wonder and awe surged through me, shattering all of my former understandings of life and love, purpose and faith. Now I knew. I knew that the one, true God was here—is here—here in the midst of rock and sand, here surrounded by blue sky and white clouds. Here, in the midst of my homesickness and longings, is the God who cannot be contained by walls, but who calls all creation home.

God's voice echoed with chords of promise and love and I knew there was no one as wonderful as this God. I heard this God's promise to free the Hebrew people—people whose blood ran through my veins. Tears of joy coursed down my cheeks, for I had never experienced a love so deep and powerful. My heart beat with a rhythm of exuberant anticipation until I heard—"Guess who is going to help me!"

I thought I was either losing my mind, caught up in some sort of wishful hallucination or this was some sort of divine, celestial joke. Wonder and awe gave way to fear and doubt. I looked into the sky. I looked down at the ground. I shuffled my feet in the sand. But God wouldn't give up. "Go and set my people free."

This sounded like a very bad idea to me. In the first place I was a wanted man. I had fled the scene of a murder. I had left a dead Egyptian in the dust. I had abandoned my mother to deal with the consequences of my violence. I had closed the door on Egyptians and Hebrews alike. If I went back to Egypt, I might as well walk straight into police head-quarters and give myself up. And in the second place . . . I had always been a better follower than a leader. In Egypt the only reason people did what I said was because I wore royal robes. In Midian . . . well, even the sheep didn't mind me very well. God said, "Lead my people to freedom," and I snorted deri-sively. Or at least I would have if I had the courage. Instead I mumbled and stammered all my excuses. God listened and God reassured me . . . sort of. God didn't say, "Nothing bad will happen to you." God did say, "I am with you. Never mind who you think you are, what matters is who I am and that I have chosen you."

I reasoned and argued with all my might, but God wouldn't give up. I'm not exactly sure what happened or why, but finally something—some hope, some courage, something—flamed up in me and I left that place a new person, ready to serve and love and follow wherever the light of this God led me. From that moment my life was not about Moses, but I became a witness to the fact that the great God of heaven and earth is here, with us always. The fire that I saw burning in a bush became a fire burning in my bones, my heart, and my spirit.

That wasn't the last time I knew the cold taste of fear, but it was the last time I allowed my fear to govern my ac-tions. Every time fear threatened to immobilize me or send me running back into familiar safety, I would look into the fire and remember. Every time I saw flames dancing, they called me forward. I kept the flame inside of me alive by prayer and hope, and God never let me down.

God was with me from Egyptian slave camps to Pharaoh's palace, from the swirling waters of the Reed Sea to the arid expanses of the desert, from valleys of disease to mountains of majesty. In each moment of the journey, the pillar of fire guided my steps and bolstered my courage. Flames of hope and promise lifted me when disappointment and despair broke my spirits, when people let me down, when I was so exhausted I didn't know which way to turn. God's sometimes gentle, sometimes demanding voice burned through the darkness and kept me going.

Moses' voice died away and the men sitting around the fire waited for something more—some pronouncement of blessing, some instruction, something. But Moses simply sat staring into the flames. The only sound was the crackling of the wood. Finally, one man took a branch and held it in the fire until it burst into flame. Holding it high, he stood and moved slowly toward the tents. And then a second man did the same. And then another and another, until the darkness was ablaze with starlight and firelight.

6

The Sky Is Falling: Jeremiah

Jeremiah 32:1–15

FOR YEARS Jeremiah had prayed for people to take him seriously. Oh, he had tried; God knows how hard he had tried. He had said and done everything he could think of to get God's message across. But his people were stubborn and proud. And now that everything he predicted had come true . . . well, he wished he had been wrong. His warnings had become reality as the people's greedy, power-hungry arrogance set them on a collision course with disaster. And still they didn't get it. Instead of returning to God, they pranced after the hollow idols of comfort and success. Instead of praising the God of their ancestors, they sang love songs to gods of military might and seductive pleasures. Jeremiah had pleaded and cajoled, shouted warnings and whispered advice but to no avail. Tirelessly and tearfully he plodded through the streets of Jerusalem searching for someone . . . any one . . . even one . . . who might join him in his quest for goodness and truth.

He still couldn't believe what his hard work had brought. His tireless commitment to justice and his passion for righteousness were responsible for his present circumstances—jailed as a traitor. As he sat in the lonely darkness of his cell, he sometimes thought if it weren't so frightening, it would be funny. Jeremiah a traitor? He was the only one who saw clearly the danger facing the people. He loved his people so much that he would not be silent, even when it cost him his freedom. Now, imprisoned in the guardhouse, Jeremiah waited helplessly for the horrors to come. It wasn't the loneliness that bothered him. He had grown used to that years before. Ever since that day God had reached down and grabbed hold of his heart, Jeremiah had known that the joy of a family was not to be his. No wife. No sons. No one to care and encourage and support him. But maybe that was just as well, for his commitment to his people left no room for anything or anyone else.

What bothered him the most was the fact that no matter what he said or did, it seemed to make no difference. Constrained by prison walls he had time to think—maybe too much time. He looked back on a life of humiliating rejection punctuated by poetic outbursts—devastating and gut wrenching cries of warning. He longed to clear his head of the dark horrors, but those visions of boiling cauldrons and rotten figs, cups of poisoned wine, and bars of iron were seared on his brain. After all the years of working to clear away the sin of his people, he could no longer see anything but corruption and decadence. He didn't fear the dreams of the night—he feared waking up and the visions that continually filled his mind.

He begged God to give him easy words to offer his people—words that would comfort and encourage. Instead—from the very beginning his cup was filled with bitterness and harsh warning; every word alienating those whose hunger for power had begun to define the people. But as much as he feared failure, as much as he dreaded the derision of the crowds, as much as he trembled at the thought of foreign oppression and exile…he feared God more. He knew that no matter how difficult the task, he would continue, for God had called and that was enough.

Day after day he sat in his cell—talking to whoever happened by. Talking to himself. Pleading. Shouting. Finally his voice died away and then he began to listen. To hear the horrors taking place around him. The daylight hours were a confusing babble of nervous officials and frantic citizens seeking passage out of the city. But the night was worse, for in the dark silence Jeremiah heard siege ramps being shifted into position, the taunts of Babylonian soldiers, the screams of those in the path of the soldiers—each night a little louder, a little closer.

Then one day he woke and knew that something had changed. It was as if hope had burned away and a gray horror filled the air. The smell of burning buildings—and a darker odor of burning flesh—worked its way through the streets, and Jeremiah knew that the end was near. The end of the city. The end of life as they knew it. Choking on smoke and anger and grief, Jeremiah huddled in a corner, praying that the nightmare would go away. Then out of the cacophony he heard a voice from his past. A voice that spoke in accents of home and family. He looked up in disbelief. "Yes, it's me," the man said. "Hanamel, your cousin. I need your help."

Lifting his hands as far as the chains permitted, Jeremiah retorted, "You can't be serious. You are the one with the money and connections. I couldn't convince people to listen to me before, and now it is just too late."

"You're the only one," Hanamel gasped. "I need to get out of town—and I want to take my sons with me. I don't have enough money to get far enough fast enough. But I do have some land—up there." He pointed to the smoke-tinged northern sky. "I need to sell my property. You are my kinsman. You have no children. Surely you have some money. Give it to me and I'll give you the land."

"You must think I'm a fool. Why would I want land that is most likely already in enemy hands? Why would I give you money for a deed which won't even be worth the papyrus it is written on?"

"Please," Hanamel begged. "Please—we are family after all." His voice died off into a painful silence.

Jeremiah wanted to scream, "Family? I have no family. The moment God called me I stood outside the family circle. I embarrassed you. I shamed you. I have not been welcome at your feasts for years. I have had to mourn the deaths of my parents and uncles from a distance, for the doors were shut in my face at their funerals. You have pretended not to know me when you passed me on the street. And now . . . now we are family?" These words threatened to explode from his heart, but even as he opened his mouth, the hand of God stopped the words in his throat.

Once again, Jeremiah knew that God was calling him to do the hard thing. Jeremiah knew the consequences of this moment. He, too, might need that money to save his own life and buy his freedom. Jeremiah talked courageously, but he tasted the bitterness of fear as well. He wanted to run and hide his head in the sand. He wanted to close his eyes and ears to what was happening. He wanted to distance himself from the horrors about to be unleashed. He wanted . . . well the same things he had always wanted—an ordinary, simple life. But as usual, God wouldn't let him alone. Down deep, in the core of his being, he heard, "This is your moment, Jeremiah. I need you to do this thing. I need you to set your own fears aside and let your trust in me be etched into the future."

And so Jeremiah did as his cousin asked. He did as God directed. Following all the legal requirements, he carefully recorded the deed of purchase. And then he had it placed in a pottery container and buried in a safe place. Now he was truly alone—family fleeing, money gone, all that was left was a worthless scrap of paper. And God.

As Hanamel scurried away, Jeremiah felt a calmness move through his body. He knew that even as the worst happened, even as Jerusalem was flattened and the people scattered like sand in the wind, God was not through with them. Someday a child digging for treasure, or a farmer planting a field, or a laborer working to lay the foundation for the restored Jerusalem—someone would dig up the container and they would know that in a time of economic collapse and military devastation there was one who trusted God. They would know that even in the darkest night the light of hope and promise was not extinguished. They would know that fear is not the last word, hope is. And as fields and houses rise out of the ashes of defeat, God's name will be praised.

Jeremiah closed his eyes and settled back to await whatever might happen. A new song replaced the dirge of destruction he had sung for so long. For he knew that a new day was coming. A day when prophets of doom and gloom would be replaced by apostles of joy and peace. A time was coming when the hearts of the people would be marked by a love that was not bound up by law but alive with the grace of God. A time was coming when God's mercy would reach out to embrace all the lost, lonely, broken sinners.

Jeremiah didn't know what the future would bring. All he knew was that the future was in God's hands and for now that would have to be enough. And he smiled.

7

Here She Is: Esther

Esther 1:1—4:17

THE MINUTE Mordecai walked through the door, Esther knew her world was about to change. It wasn't just the set of his jaw or the tension in his shoulders, but the oh-so- slight trembling of his hands that gave him away. Even as he began to speak, her knees gave way and she sank unto the cushion under the window. Unable to meet the intensity of his eyes, she lowered hers and waited, hardly daring to breathe.

"The queen is gone," he blurted. "She insulted the king in front of his friends, and no one can survive that sort of insubordinate behavior. Now the king is on the prowl for another—a beautiful woman with enough intelligence to be interesting, and smart enough not to show it. Esther—that woman is you."

"No," she wanted to scream. "No—I won't do it. I won't step into that arena of intrigue and corruption." But even as she opened her mouth to protest, Mordecai implored,

"Listen to me. You are beautiful. You are kind and wise. Your people need you. We need someone in high places to look out for our interests."

Esther knew that she had no real choice. Ever since her parents died, Mordecai had looked after her. He had fulfilled the legal requirements of a guardian and done it all with a loving respect that she could not ignore. If Mordecai needed her to do this . . .

Esther nodded her head.

Everything after that was a blur. It was only as they stood just outside the palace gate that Mordecai offered his final piece of advice, "Esther, dear child. You are beautiful and wise and kind, but you are also a Hebrew. And that could work against you. Be yourself in every way but this— keep your family background a secret."

That was when the fear took hold, for secret keeping is a fearsome thing. One slip of the tongue, and she could suffer the fate of so many who crossed the king. But it was too late to change her mind. Mordecai slipped away as the king's eunuch ushered her into the chamber set aside for her use. Weeks went by. Weeks of grooming and training. Weeks of kid-glove treatment. Weeks of loneliness. Weeks that dragged by. And then everything shifted into fast forward. Audience with the king. Marriage. Coronation. As the crown was set onto her head, Esther's shoulders sank and it was all she could do to hold back her sobs.

As time passed, she adapted to her new life, but the fear never left her. She trusted her servants—up to a point. Hathach in particular possessed an air of kind consideration. But she knew that their loyalty could vanish once they learned that she was a Jew. The only person she could trust totally was Mordecai, and every conversation with him ran the risk of being overheard. Day after day, week after week, she buried her identity deeper and deeper beneath layers of court protocol. While her fear never left her, she managed to keep it under control. Almost. Except for the hours just after the sun set, when shadows gathered and crept their way into her heart. In the gathering darkness she often sat in the corner of her room, wrapped in a shawl woven from red and purple threads—the only thing she had that belonged to her life before her coronation. As she pulled it around her she smelled the scent of home. That was the only thing that kept her sane when fear of discovery and betrayal edged its way into her heart.

She was glad that when her fears were realized it was in the heat of the day. For in the harsh light of the noonday sun, it was somehow easier to act with courage. She was sitting in the courtyard when the eunuch bringing her tea, said, "Did you hear what that fool Mordecai has done now?"

Esther took a cooling swallow, letting the liquid ease her throat so she could speak calmly, "Mordecai?"

"Yes," her servant snorted. "Mordecai the Jew. Thinks he is so much better than anyone—refusing to bow down to the king was bad enough, but now . . . he is going around creating a public spectacle of himself. His days are numbered believe you me."

Esther felt a trickle of sweat roll down her side and she fanned herself with her shawl as she said in as calm a voice as she could muster, "What do you mean creating a spectacle? I thought he was a good Jew."

"Good," exclaimed her servant! "Good? There is no such thing as a good Jew. It's about time we got rid of every last one of them. And we will, too. Mordecai thinks his crocodile tears will soften the king's heart, but he might as well save his tears—he'll need them soon enough."

"You're not making sense," Esther blurted out. "Get rid of every Jew? There is no way."

"You really haven't heard, have you? The final solution is already in motion and a year from now every one of those nasty Jews—every man, woman, and child will be killed, destroyed, and exterminated like the rats they are."

Esther felt as if her heart would explode, but she forced down her rising panic. Moving with deliberate calm she entered into the quiet of the inner room and there she found Hathach. Clenching her hands to still their trembling, she took a leap of faith that left her breathless. She sent Hathach to Mordecai. "Ask him," she said. Ask him what he thinks he is doing. Tell him that I beg him to stop."

The minute Hathach left, Esther felt the fear rising in her until she thought she would drown. What if? What if Hathach went straight to the king and told him Esther was seeking contact with a Jew? She pulled her shawl around her and sank to the floor where she waited. The next few hours were the longest of Esther's life. When Hathach returned, however, the look in his eyes was so filled with pity that she began to tremble all the more.

"I found Mordecai," he said, "and he sent you a message." Hathach paused as if he were struggling to keep from crying. "He said for me to tell you that all of the Jews are doomed. There is only one chance—for you to go to the king and plead for them."

Not daring to meet Hathach's eyes, Esther looked down at her hands. Then, talking in a voice so low he had to strain to hear, she whispered. "Tell Mordecai what he asks of me is impossible. I can't go to the king uninvited—no one can. His anger is terrifying and if he chooses he can have the uninvited interloper killed. Tell him to remember what happened the last time a queen acted in opposition to the king. I can do nothing."

Hathach reached out a pitying hand as if to touch her cheek, but as quickly pulled it back and left again. Now Esther's fear began simmering with guilt and despair—a bitter stew of self-loathing. It wasn't long before Hathach returned. This time, he spoke in a voice that carried the tone of her dear cousin. "Esther," he said, "do you really think your life will be spared? You are one of us, you know. If you remain silent, deliverance will appear, and you will know that you could have done something and didn't. And that will kill your spirit. Esther, it just may be that it is for this that you have been made queen. It just may be that this is the moment for which you have been created. It just may be that you are the one God needs."

With each word, Esther felt an infusion of courage and at last she looked straight into Hathach's eyes seeing in them a reflection of the cousin who had cared for her when she was so alone. She saw the men and women and children who would die if she did nothing. And she knew that even death at the hand of the king was better than living with the knowledge that she could have done something and didn't. Fear was no match for that knowledge. "Pray for me," she finally said. "Pray for me."

And she prepared to answer the call. Later, as she tried to remember, it was all a blur of confusing color, of raised voices, a hushed silence, and an ocean of relief that swept through her as her people were spared. The only thing she could remember clearly was the look of pride on Mordecai's face as she stood before the king.

She often thought about that time and the way fear had worked its damaging power into the nation. Fear had turned one group of people against another. Fear had cast a blanket of darkness over the land. Fear had turned power into a holocaust of evil. But, each time someone spoke out in protest, each time someone offered love in the face of hate, each time someone refused to go along with bigotry, a thread of goodness was stitched into the tapestry of life. Her thread didn't seem like much, but in the end, it held the fabric of a people together.

8

A Blessed Event: Elizabeth

Luke 1:5–25, 39–45

NUMBNESS WAS a relief after decades of agonizing pain and bitter disappointment. Elizabeth sometimes looked back on her early years and shook her head at the foolish girl she had been. How many hours she had wasted, staring into the clouds and imagining her future—wedding festivities and then the joy of children. It was a wonder that any man wanted her, given her penchant for dreaming. Her poetry was much better than her cooking. But, according to plan, Zechariah appeared. While he wasn't exactly the dashing man of her dreams, he was good and kind, as practical as she was not. He took everything seriously—somehow managing to follow the rules imposed by Rome as well as those instituted by Yahweh. As they began their life together, Elizabeth found her heart touched by Zechariah's quiet kindnesses and gentle smile. Their families were both pleased with the match and anticipated children blessed with Zechariah's common sense and Elizabeth's zest for life.

The sense of letting her family down made Elizabeth's barrenness all the more painful. Month after month went by with no sign of life stirring in her. At first she was not too upset. God was good and so she waited patiently for God to give her sons and daughters. But the empty months became empty years, and at last Elizabeth's anticipation turned to desperation.

Everywhere she looked she saw women with swollen stomachs and self-satisfied smiles. She began to flinch every time she heard a baby cry, but she kept a brave face in public. Only when she was alone did she let her defenses drop. She prayed all the time. Anguished prayers of supplication. Hopeful, pleading prayers. Outraged, demanding prayers. Prayers that resulted in only an empty silence. Prayers born out of the fear that she would die a failure—arms as empty as her womb.

But even as heartache grew, she kept busy. For a while she even found a bit of contentment and companionship as she met the neighbors at the well, where they exchanged gossip and advice as they filled their buckets with water. As a young girl, Elizabeth loved this time, the cool splash of the water in the jar, the hum of conversation punctuated by giggles and sometimes screams of delight as good news was shared. As a newlywed, she turned to these same women for advice about everything from preparing a savory stew to recognizing the signs of pregnancy. But as time went on and those signs failed to materialize, Elizabeth began to dread water gathering. She cringed as the chattering women snuck surreptitious glances at her all-too-flat belly. The last straw came one spring morning. Her neighbor, a toddler clinging to her skirt and a newborn cradled in her arm, grumbled to the women filling the water jars, "This one cries all the time and this one demands all my attention, and now another one is on the way."

"Oh, but you are so blessed," Elizabeth began.

"Well," her neighbor snapped, "if you think this is such a blessing, why don't you try it yourself."

Those words triggered a flood of grief deep inside—wave after wave of sadness and pain and fear. Fear that she would never have a baby, fear that God had turned away from her, fear that she was not worthy of a blessing, fear that everyone was laughing at her. Tears choked her and she turned and quickly walked home. That was the last time she went to the well with the other women.

That moment at the well marked a turning point for Elizabeth. She took her precious dreams and folded them up and buried them deep inside herself. She wrapped up her feelings—the joy, the sadness, the hope, the anger—and set them aside. Life was easier that way—no emotion, no pain. No hopefulness, no fear. She took her energy and put it to good, practical use. She cooked and cleaned. She cared for her husband. She cared for her neighbors—but no one ever saw her smile or cry again.

Years passed like this—duty fulfilled, responsibilities completed. So the time passed as Elizabeth and Zechariah worked hard, talked little, and stifled their dreams. Then one day, Zechariah returned from temple duty and even before she saw him, Elizabeth knew something had happened. He wasn't trudging along the path, but running and stumbling and gasping for air. Some of the other men were with him, which was a good thing, for every time he tried to speak he choked on his words. Finally, one of them burst out, "He's been like that ever since he came out of the temple. His face was all shiny and his hands trembled and yet he couldn't say a word."

Even this change in her husband didn't disturb Elizabeth's equilibrium. The house was quieter, but Elizabeth just kept on with her routine. She refused to allow herself to feel anything—but a few weeks later her body began behaving oddly. She was sleepy all the time, and began having trouble keeping food in her stomach. "If I didn't know better," she thought, "I would think . . . No. No. Impossible." But when her waistline expanded and she began to feel quickening movements in her womb, she knew. "Why now?" she agonized. "I'm too old. Surely, God is teasing me, offering life only to snatch it away."

With each new sign of pregnancy, Elizabeth became more frightened. She refused to set herself up for a disappointment that would surely kill her, and so she drew herself deeper and deeper into an isolating shell of stoicism. Five months passed and the rains came—the gray, wet weather matching Elizabeth's state of mind. She sat in the corner mending Zechariah's robe when the door burst open and a young girl stood staring at her. "It's me," she said, "Mary your cousin. Is it true? Are you really pregnant?"

Elizabeth's heart leapt into her throat. It was as if a wall had tumbled down, a stone rolled away from the tomb of despair in which she had buried herself. Pregnant? She was. She was pregnant. "I am," she sang out. "I am going to have a baby." She felt the darkness roll back in the face of a flood of light and color—all the colors of the rainbow. A light that came not from the sky, but from Mary herself, filled the air with beauty. Words burst from Elizabeth, words pent up for years, words of joy and gladness that seemed to go on and on. "I see the future," she sang. "Your son will be the hope of the world and mine will be a part of that great day when all will live in love. The dream is about to come true and you and I and all the generations to come will be caught up in grace. Day after day will unfold with adventure and purpose and we have a part to play. You, Mary, and me, Elizabeth, need not fear, for God can do anything."

For four months, that song of hope sustained Elizabeth. She and Mary spent hours talking and laughing, imagining the future their sons would share. She watched Mary swell with new life, she watched her own waistline expand and she finally allowed herself to look to the future with a sense of confidence. Even when Mary left to return to her own home, Elizabeth was sustained by what they shared.

Her pains began late one evening. Gentle cramping at first, but soon it was a relentless grinding misery. Zechariah tried to comfort her . . . awkwardly patting her on the arm with each contraction. Then, just when she thought that she could bear it no longer, the cloth hanging across her room was pushed aside and three of her neighbors stood there. One shepherded Zechariah out of the room, one laid a cool cloth on Elizabeth's forehead, and the third began encouraging Elizabeth, guiding her breathing. At last with one mighty push, Elizabeth's son took a breath and burst into an outraged cry.

"He's a noisy one, all right," one of the women said. "Here Elizabeth, don't you want to hold little Zechariah?"

Elizabeth reached out her arms to embrace the wriggling baby, "His name," she said, "is John."

The women exchanged puzzled glances. Surely Zechariah would want his son named after himself. One of the women bustled out to find the new father who must have been pacing right outside the door, for in seconds he was standing by his wife. "Welcome, John," he whispered. "Welcome, John."

Elizabeth lay there and for the first time in her life she was utterly content. Oh, she knew that the days and weeks and months ahead would be difficult. She was not young and this child would demand much from her. She knew that disease and accident waited to ensnare her baby. She knew that his life would be difficult and harsh. But she also knew that God was a God of wonder and might. She knew that there was nothing that God could not do. She knew that her job now was to instill in the infant now nursing at her breast, a single-minded devotion to God. Her work was to love John—and to create in him a passion for serving God, the courage to speak out for what was right, and a fearless stance toward the future. And when Mary's child was born . . . well, Elizabeth wasn't sure just what would happen, but she knew that God was at work. No matter what happened, she knew that she would never be afraid again.

9

In the Still of the Night: Joseph

Matthew 1:18—2:23

MIND YOUR own business. Do your job well. Keep a low profile. Follow the rules. Those were the tenets of Joseph's life—tenets that served him well. Even as a young boy, Joseph could be counted on to finish his chores before running off to play with the other children. As he grew and matured, the women in the village took note of his strong arms and gentle eyes, more than one marking him as good son-in-law material. Joseph was reliable and law-abiding, a good man who worked hard and slept the sleep of one whose conscience was untroubled.

Now, after years of hard work, Joseph's steady responsibility had finally paid off and he was able to afford the wife and family for which his heart had yearned so long. Mary was her name and her sweet gentleness was a perfect match for Joseph's stable devotion to duty. Mary and Joseph. Even the women at the well had to agree that this was a match made in heaven. After the arrangements were made, Joseph worked with a new lightness of spirit. Until . . . until his life was sent spinning into chaos and confusion.

Usually he began smiling the minute he heard the staccato rhythm of Mary's feet against the hard-pressed dirt—almost as if she were dancing her way into the next encounter, the next glimpse of beauty or joy. But this morning hesitancy marked her steps. Listening, Joseph felt the bottom drop out of his stomach and very slowly he lay down his hammer and lifted his head. Mary stood in the doorway, her features a blur against the bright sunlit background.

"Mary, what . . . what is it?" he stuttered, trying to keep the panic from his voice.

"Oh, Joseph." Mary's voice sounded as if it were coming from far beneath the water—all choked and muffled. "Oh, Joseph . . . try to understand."

He did. He tried. But none of it made sense. Pregnant? There was no way he was the father. Even though he ached to hold Mary, to caress her . . . he had held back. Out of respect for Mary, out of obedience to the law, he had refused to give in to the longings of his heart. And now? Now the woman he loved was carrying someone else's child. It was more than he could bear. Mary was still talking, but Joseph stumbled from the room, seeking to get as far away from her as he could before the pain burst out of his chest in one long, agonizing cry.

He ran as far and as fast as he could, finally collapsing near a small stream of water. One moment, one conversation, and his life had turned upside down and inside out. All his life he had lived in ways that would keep him out of trouble and now he was in trouble anyway. The law was clear—get Mary out of his life quickly and completely.

Divorce her or kill her. Either option was right and legal. But Joseph knew that either one would destroy him. He was terrified, for if the law was not the answer, he had no clue what the answer was. The very foundation on which he had so carefully erected his life was crumbling and he was falling into an abyss of sadness and fear. Head pounding he wept until he could weep no more, and finally he fell asleep.

Minutes passed, hours, days . . . he wasn't sure how long he had slept. He did know that he was not the same man when he awoke. He could never articulate what had happened, all he knew was that when he fell asleep he was filled with fear. When he awoke, woven through his doubts and anger, were threads of hope and promise. Sometimes in the spring, the wind rustled the olive trees in a way that made his pulse race and his heart leap with anticipation. That was just the way he felt now and he didn't understand it. The heartache of Mary's news seemed to have melted away, leaving him stronger and more sure of love than he had ever been. He hurried off to tell Mary that he was ready to stand with her against any mean-spirited gossip, any finger-pointing criticism. Joseph and Mary and . . . Well, there would be time enough to get used to the fact that his family would be coming much sooner than he had thought. But, somehow he wasn't afraid anymore.

The next few months passed by in a blur. Mary packed her bags and hustled out of town right after Joseph's promise to stick by her. But Joseph didn't mind. He had more than enough work to keep him busy and he needed the time to think about all that had happened. He was actually relieved when word came that he was going to have to go to Bethlehem with Mary for the census. It would give the two of them some time alone, and if the baby were born away from home, well . . . it would spare Mary the self-righteous clucking of the town busy-bodies who were all too quick to sniff out hints of scandal.

It was a long journey. Joseph hadn't counted on the number of stops a pregnant woman needed to make or the slowness with which she moved. When they got to Bethlehem, the last rays of the sun had already faded away. A cold breeze was blowing and Joseph was relieved to find shelter for the night—even if it was a rough and rugged stable. Warmed by the body heat of the animals, Mary and Joseph had just nestled into the straw when Mary's sharp gasp jolted him upright. From that moment on things moved quickly, the quiet of the night transformed into a symphony of lowing cattle and clucking hens accompanied by Mary's moans and grunts, and finally a long, loud note of victory sounding from a tiny baby.

Joseph was ready. He was ready to support Mary, to provide for her and the child. At least he hoped he was. Or was he? Ever since he learned that Mary was going to have a baby, Joseph had wondered how he would feel when he saw him. At the moment of birth, Joseph knew that he was supposed to hold the child and give him a name—thus claiming paternity in a public and irrevocable manner. Joseph knew that was what he would do if the child were his. But this was, after all, not his child. When he had thought about it, Joseph had worried that when the time came, he might not have the courage for that sort of public acknowledgement. Joseph had been so busy he hadn't had time to feel anything, but as the child's cry pierced the night, he felt an explosion of light and love rising up from deep within.

Scooping the child into his arms, and wrapping him in a soft blanket he looked into the child's eyes and all doubt and fear fled. "This is Jesus," he murmured. And then in a voice that rang through the courtyard, "This is Jesus!"

At first Joseph thought he would never sleep again—between Jesus' needs and the constant stream of visitors, there was little chance for rest. But as Jesus settled into the rhythm of life, Joseph discovered that it wasn't the midnight cries of hunger that bothered him. It wasn't the endless chatter of visitors. It was the times of silence that bothered him the most. Sometimes he would quietly rest his hand on the child's back to feel the slight movement that meant his baby was still breathing. His baby—that was the way he thought of him and it was only in the deepest darkness of night that he remembered and quivered with fear.

Joseph had just begun to feel as if his feet were on solid ground when the rumors began. His uneasiness was heightened as he listened to the stories spilling from the palace. At first there were jokes about Herod's paranoia, but it didn't take long for the laughter to die away. The sense of impending disaster began to weigh heavily on Joseph. He tried to ignore it, to carry on with life as usual. But the massacre at the market was too much. He was on his way back to Mary and Jesus when he saw a woman carrying a small bundle darting her way through the crowds, followed by one of the palace guards. As she neared Joseph she tripped over a corner of the fish-seller's tent and the bundle slid from her hands and was scooped up by the guard. Her scream lodged itself in Joseph's brain—a crescendo of rage and pain—but what he would never forget was the look on the guard's face as he choked the life from the tiny infant. Joseph was close enough to look into the guard's eyes and what he saw there haunted him forever. For he saw . . . nothing. No spark of humanity, no shred of regret, not even victory. Even as Joseph reached out to help, to grab the baby, it was over. The woman crouched by her dead child and the guard melted away into the crowd. Joseph never remembered how he got back to Mary and Jesus. He tried to keep the story from Mary, to shelter his family as long as he could, but Mary knew that something was wrong. Even Jesus seemed to pick up Joseph's anxiety. He clung to Mary and she paced up and down the small room for hours in a futile effort to lull him to sleep. She finally laid him on a blanket and curled her body around his. Their sleep-filled breathing was a relief to Joseph, giving him quiet to think. But sleep eluded him as he tossed and turned for hours. Finally, just as the sun peeked above the horizon, he dozed a bit. It was in that state of suspended animation—not quite awake, not fully asleep—that he heard it. A soft whisper moving through his head and his heart. "Joseph," it said, "don't be afraid. You mustn't stay here. Get up now and take Mary and her baby and get out of town. Go to Egypt."

Joseph opened his mouth to protest—not Egypt! Not the place of his people's nightmarish slavery! Not the land of pyramids and foreign gods. But the voice was insistent. "Go now, Joseph. Trust God and do not be afraid."

Once again, Joseph laid his fear aside and moved forward. He gathered his small family and set out to a new life in a strange place. It was only when the wind blew from the north carrying with it the smells of the sea, or when a merchant spoke in the familiar accents of Judah, that Joseph felt his heart ache with longing and loss. He refused, however to let his homesickness hold him back. He managed to put his carpentry skills to good use. He and Mary began to make a home and Jesus, well Jesus was the delight of Joseph's life. Finally he was happy. Finally his fears had been put to rest. Finally he had his life figured out and then . . . he slept. He went to bed one night with the plans for his life all laid out, and he woke up with these plans crumbled at his feet. "Go home," the voice said. "It is time. It's safe. I need you to take the child back to his people." And so, once again, Joseph became a man on the move, setting aside his own fears and doubts, his own agenda, to follow God.

Sometimes Joseph would chuckle quietly to himself when he heard the other men complain about the challenges of raising a family. If they only knew, he would think. After the roller coaster ride of those years, nothing was beyond him. And so the years flew by. Years of steadily and quietly working with his tools to provide for his family. Years of talking with Jesus, teaching him, preparing him for the responsibilities of adulthood. And at the end, as Joseph lay breathing his last the voice came again. "Dear Joseph," it said, "don't be afraid. You are a good and righteous man. You have served me faithfully. Well done, my friend. Well done."

10

He Touched Me: A Leper

Mark 1:40–45

IT WAS his favorite time of day . . . that time when the sun's light faded away and the cool night breeze blew across the rooftop. He stretched his legs and rested his back on the pillow his daughter had brought up when she brought him his evening cup of wine. Then the peaceful silence was shattered as a small girl darted up the ladder and across the roof. "I hate my life," she cried. "Look at me. My arm is so shriveled up the other children say I am worthless and they won't let me play with them. Miriam actually ran away when she saw me coming and said that her mother told her to stay away from me, that I must have done something really bad for God to punish me with a withered arm. Why can't I be like the other children?"

The man smiled at the trembling child and patted the ground near his feet. "I know what you are going through," he began. "Don't be afraid. Let me tell you my story. Maybe that will help." As the little girl curled up beside him, he began.

Whenever my story is told, I am always referred to as *leper*—and that one word says it all. I was no longer a person, but a thing—a thing to be feared and avoided. Sticks and stones may break my bones, but names can never hurt me—that's how the old childhood rhyme went, but each time I heard, "Leper, leper go away. Never welcome night or day," I felt as if I had suffered a direct hit. Names may not break bones, but they do bruise the soul. Leprosy was a horrible disease, but the worst part was the fear. Fear that the curses defined me. Fear that I was as worthless as everyone said. Fear that this torturous agony affecting body and soul would not even end with my death, but that even in Sheol I would be isolated and alone.

I wasn't always a leper, you know. Years ago I had a name, work to do, people who loved me. And then it all changed. At first I tried to ignore the white patches appearing on my skin. Then I tried to wash them off. To invent excuses for the flaking scales. To cover them up. But eventually I had to face the truth. I was a leper. Unclean. Impure. My family pretended not to notice, for they knew as well as I did that leprosy was a death sentence—not just a physical death, but a death of the future. No more human contact. No more dreams. Only shame and loneliness and suffering.

Even as the creeping blemishes moved over my skin, we never talked about it; hoping that if we ignored it, it would just go away. But I never quit thinking about it. I had been taught that leprosy was a direct result of some great sin—a punishment from God, so to speak. In the dark hours of the night I tossed and turned on my pallet as I tried to figure out what I had done wrong, how I had displeased God. I knew I had made mistakes. I had said hurtful words. I had not always been faithful in my prayers. But this seemed a heavy burden to bear for my actions. I began to fear that I was such a horrid person that my very presence was an affront to God, and this was God's way of destroying a flawed member of creation.

I agonized and worried until one day as I went to worship with my family, the priest met us at the door, blocking my way with outstretched arms. He stood there, his eyes not quite meeting mine, and in a loud voice recited from the book of Leviticus, "The person who has the leprous disease shall wear torn clothes and let the hair of his head be disheveled. And he shall cover his upper lip and cry out, 'Unclean, Unclean.'" (Lev 13:45) Each word was like a slap in the face hitting me with the reality of the disease, the reality of my brokenness, and I knew that I had just heard my funeral sermon. My heart still beat, but now I was dead. All those gathered began to back away from me as they shouted horrible things—vile names dripping with hate and fear. Sticks and stones can break your bones, but words can destroy. I had no choice. With one last glance at the tear-stained faces of my family, I walked away to join the roving bands of decaying men and women who haunted the shadows.

And then the nightmare began. It's hard for me to talk about even now. There is no way to explain the horror of watching one's own body waste away. A sick fear met me each morning as I opened my eyes and saw people who looked just like I would in a few months or years: gaping wounds, rashes, peeling skin. We looked like grotesque distortions of human beings. No one to care for us. No one to hug or touch us. No one to call us by name. We were only *leper.*

Can you even imagine what it feels like? Whenever another human being was near, as if our torn clothes and disheveled hair wasn't an obvious enough sign, those of us who still had lips were compelled to call out, "Unclean! Unclean!" I am ugly. I am worthless. I am garbage. We weren't even able to walk on the fringes of society, for as soon as they heard us children would scurry away; men would look at us as if we were cockroaches or other nasty vermin; women would cross the road and avert their eyes. My ears rang with taunts and laughter, and cries of *monster, freak, sinner.* I knew how bad I looked, how disgusting and strange. But I also knew that underneath the oozing sores I was still me. I hungered for someone to see that. I longed for someone to say, "You are a human being precious in the eyes of God. You matter in the great scheme of things. You are part of God's creation, shaped by God's hands, loved by God. Let me help you. Let me love you." But I feared . . . I knew . . . that would never happen. Instead I fed on a constant diet of rejection and humiliation and hostility.

At first some of us found comfort in each other's presence. Under starlit skies we would remember back when we were somebodies, when we laughed and worked, when we loved and were loved. But after awhile, the memories became too painful, too distant. More and more I kept to myself. I prayed . . . a lot. I threw questions into the sky: "Why are you doing this to me? If you are a God of love, why can't you love me? Am I so bad?" Eventually, worn down by the silence, I gave up and simply sank into my misery. Months passed and it was not only my body that was disintegrating—my heart was so dried up, I sometimes feared it had already stopped beating and I had become a walking dead man.

Then stories about an unusual rabbi who was healing began filtering down to us through snippets of overheard conversations. As I heard about demons cast out and blind eyes opened and limbs straightened, I felt the faintest breath of hope. Maybe, I thought, just maybe this Jesus might have a word for me. And so one day I set out to find him. I knew the risk. It was highly likely that the crowd would kill me before I could even get close to him. But I ask you. What would you have done? The truth is I was more afraid of living than of dying.

At first I hoped to sneak my way into his presence. Maybe the torn clothing and matted, tangled hair wouldn't be noticed if I were quiet enough. But as I got near to him, the crowds became thicker and thicker and I knew I had no chance of getting close enough for him to notice me. Then I had an idea. "Unclean! Unclean!" I yelled. The crowds parted before me like the Reed Sea. Only one man stood his ground and didn't pull away, and I knew that this was the one I had heard so much about. Muttered curses and hate-filled shouts filled the air, but I kept my attention focused on this Jesus.

The words came hard to my lips, for it had been years since I had spoken much besides "unclean," but this was my only chance. "Please," I stuttered, "please, if you choose you can make me clean." And I waited for him to speak. Finally I lifted my head to look at him. What I noticed was his eyes—staring at the crowd, he silenced them with the force of what seemed like anger. Anger directed not at me, but at them. Staring at them until their horrible words died away.

I began to tremble. Could it be true? Could this holy man really care about outcasts? Could he possibly be angry about the rejection and hurt inflicted on any human being . . . even a leper? And then he looked at me. I couldn't move. I couldn't breathe. His eyes softened and I knew that he wasn't looking *at* me; he was looking *into* me. He saw the aching loneliness, the longing for acceptance, the fear of rejection. He saw my wounded, bleeding spirit. I waited for him to speak, to say, "I wish I could help you, but only God can heal one as awful as you." Or "confess your sin and you will be healed." I waited there in all my ugliness and then the unbelievable happened. He touched me. He touched me. It had been so long. I had forgotten how warm a human hand could be. My heart swelled until I thought it might burst with joy. Outwardly I stood in silence, but inside I was shouting, "Yes—I am a human being. Yes—I am precious in the eyes of God. Yes—I matter. Yes—I am a child of God."

It wasn't until I heard the gasp of the crowd that I looked at my skin. It was clear. I had prayed for that for years, but now that it happened, I realized that as important as that was, the true miracle was that this man, despite the taunts and taboos of the community laid his hand on me . . . one rejected and despised.

I could hear his voice telling me something about priests and inspections, but the singing in my heart was so loud that nothing else seemed to matter. I practically danced my way through the crowd; telling anyone who would listen, "Look at my arm. Look at my face. He touched me. God loves me. God loves you. God loves us all. Alleluia. Alleluia."

I've thought about that moment a lot. The healing of my body was wonderful, but what really matters is that Jesus erased my fear and I learned that there was nothing so terrible, so disgusting, so frightening that God would turn away. Just as a caterpillar becomes a butterfly, so I was transformed from a leper into a child of God.

With that the man's voice quieted a moment and then he placed his arm around the small body huddled at his feet. "Don't be afraid, child," he crooned. God sees you and loves you, too. The touch of Jesus opened my ears to the song of God that sings through the days and nights of even ones such as you and me. Listen and hear it.

And in the quiet place of her heart, the little girl heard, "I know you child. I know all about you. Let me touch you and be with you in your pain. I am always with you. In joy I am with you. In suffering and shadows I am with you. Don't hide from me, but let me hold you close. In my sight you are perfection. I am your God who breathed into you the breath of life. I love you." For a moment she just sat and then, hugging the leper she whispered, "Thank you, Grandpa. I love you, too."

11

Sons of Thunder: Zebedee's Wife

Matthew 20:17-23, 27:50-56

THE MINUTE Zebedee walked in the door, his wife knew that something horrible had happened. Zebedee usually announced his entrance with an explosion of words. If the day had gone well, his booming laughter echoed off the walls. If the day had gone badly, the air resounded with curses and expletives that she had learned to ignore. Zebedee was a good man whose emotions were quickly vented and just as quickly forgotten. This day had started off as usual with Zebedee and their sons James and John heading out to work just as the sun peeked over the horizon. The wind carried with it the threat of a storm, so instead of risking the watery tumult, they planned to catch up on some repairs. Zebedee was a bit impatient about this change of plans, as he loved nothing as much as meeting the challenge of wind and wave, but his sons had persuaded him that nets needed to be mended. He grumbled a bit as they walked off, but his wife knew that this day at least, she need not worry about their safety on a stormy sea.

She busied herself with chores until, just as she was getting ready to carry some bread and olives to them for their lunch, Zebedee shuffled into the room. One look at his face and her heart seemed to stop. He was quiet. No swearing. No laughing. He sat—staring out the door. "What is it?" she whispered. "Are you hurt? Are the boys hurt?" His silence spun her into a dark place and her voice rose, "What is it?" she demanded. "Talk to me!" He shifted his eyes toward her face for a moment and then looked at the floor.

"They just walked away," he whispered. "They threw the nets down and just walked away." His wife felt a scream rising up from the pit of her stomach. "What are you talking about? Look at me." But Zebedee just shook his head and disappeared somewhere so deep inside himself that she couldn't touch him. Oh, he walked and he talked. He ate what she set in front of him, but it was as if all the life and spirit had drained away. This man who laughed in the face of dangerous storms, this man who never let any human being frighten or intimidate him, this man of thundering passions had come face to face with a situation he couldn't control, and he crumbled.

Zebedee's wife was afraid for her husband and her sons, and this fear led her to action. She marched down to the rocky coast and straight up to the men who were sitting there. It was these men who told her what had happened. They talked about a man named Jesus who had swept through their group, leaving them shaken and expectant and confused. She never discovered exactly what he had said, only that his words were so powerful, his presence so charismatic, that when he left, four of the fishermen, including her sons, left with him.

That day her life turned upside down. She had always assumed that her sons would remain near her; that life would go on in its familiar patterns. Instead, she was left with an empty shell of a husband and sons who moved in and out of her life. Each morning she awoke with a knot of fear in the pit of her stomach. Fear that one day her sons would not return. Fear for their safety and for her own. She tried to keep a positive attitude, but every time one of her friend's sons got married, every time one of the women became a grandmother, she choked back tears of regret and disappointment.

She was somewhat comforted by the fact that, at least at first, their new responsibilities kept them near enough to home that she was able to see them periodically. And, as hard as it was to admit, when she was with them, she saw more joy and peace than she had ever seen before. She looked for opportunities to observe and listen to Jesus, and over the months she felt her fear recede. His message of forgiveness and mercy, his compassion and tenderness, his refusal to be defeated by any doubt or danger—like a gentle rain that soaks the earth, his teachings worked in her heart until she felt courage and hope blossom.

Then the earth shifted beneath her once again. James came to her one warm spring morning and told her that they were leaving Galilee and going to Jerusalem. A cold chill washed over her, for she knew that of all the places they should not go, Jerusalem was the worst. Even in Galilee, they had been hearing rumblings from the powers that be in the Temple. Those in control wanted to stay in control, and Jesus' messages of new beginnings, of a freedom to live out of love rather than being bound by restrictive regulations that stifled love, had already led to angry conflict. So far the conflict was limited to words, but she feared that soon the bitter words would lead to worse. Resistance to Jesus was mounting and, while the ordinary people flocked to hear him, he had no friends in high places. Jerusalem . . . she was terrified. She reached out to grab James' hand, but he stepped back and shook his head sadly. And she knew that she had to let them go.

She looked at Zebedee, longing for him to say something. Do something. But he just stared straight ahead, and then she knew what she had to do. The only way she could protect her sons was to stay with them. And if they insisted on leaving, she had only one option—go with them. She grabbed her cloak and gathered together as much food as she could fit into her bag, and off she went She caught up with the group just as they paused for the night. John was the first to see her, and she almost laughed, for his eye-rolling expression reminded her of the look he gave her when he was a teen-ager. This time, however, the look of frustrated impatience quickly faded. He smiled and nodded toward a small group of women sitting by the fire. She quickly joined them and as they shifted to make room for her, one of them grabbed her hand and gave it a squeeze.

The days seemed to fly by—long dusty walks punctuated by moments of such beauty that she almost couldn't bear the wonder of it all. Even as fear gripped her, these moments, like stars flickering in the night, helped her see the goodness of it all. One time, in particular, fed her spirit for days. Trudging along the rocky trail, the little band had only one thought . . . rest. They longed for a cool stream and soft grass. Then they rounded a bend and almost as one they groaned. Coming toward them were dozens of men and women and she knew that rest would have to wait. And when she saw that this delegation was led by some Pharisees, her heart sank. She couldn't hear what was said, but their body language told her all she needed to know. The Pharisees with jaws clenched as tightly as their fists, Jesus hands open and slightly extended as if ready to embrace.

Then, just as the Pharisees turned and stalked away, some women moved in. And not just women, but children too. She wanted to weep with frustration. They didn't have time for this. Jesus was tired. She scanned the crowd and finally caught James' eyes. And James knew what she wanted. He stepped in to try and divert the women, to spare Jesus and get them moving, But Jesus held up his hand. He looked at the children—the little girl with tangled hair and big eyes, the toddler giggling as he strutted along, the boy with the gap-toothed grin. He saw the bruised and trembling ones, the dancing and babbling ones. She would never forget what happened next. Jesus face shone with the biggest smile she had ever seen. Light seemed to radiate from him and his arms seemed to grow until his hug embraced the whole bunch of them. "Don't discourage them," he whispered. "Let them come closer, for God's love is for them." And she knew. She knew that Jesus understood the love of parent and child. He knew the delight a mother felt when she watched a baby's first steps. He knew a father's pride over a child's quick wit. He knew the love that would sacrifice anything for the beloved.

That understanding was so surprising, that she didn't even think—she just moved up to Jesus. "Consider my sons," she said. "They are good boys. They have worked hard and sacrificed everything. Let them have key places in your kingdom—one at your right and one at your left." Jesus looked at her with a look of such pity and understanding, that the harshness of his words were softened. "You have no idea what you ask," he said. "Haven't you been listening? The cup I will drink is life giving, but to drink it is to enter into a way of life that requires all you have. Your sons will know the peace and joy of this life, but striving for position is not the way."

He continued to speak about serving and greatness, but she couldn't listen any more. Confused and ashamed, she slipped toward the back of the group, trying to stay unnoticed for the rest of the journey. All too soon they were in Jerusalem and there her personal embarrassment was washed away by the horrors of her worst nightmare come true. Evil crouched in every corner and darkness swept across her soul as she watched Jesus those last days. Even the Passover celebration was tainted by a sense of impending doom. As soon as Jesus and the disciples left, she and the other women began cleaning the room. She picked up the cup that Jesus had used to share the wine and held it to her lips. Closing her eyes, she inhaled the aroma of grapes and let it seep into her soul. She tasted the last few drops and felt love course through her body.

Later she was thankful that she had that moment, that feeling, to hang on to as the bottom dropped out of her world, for it was all that kept fear from devouring her through Jesus' arrest and trial. She didn't know which was worse—looking at Jesus' suffering or looking at the empty eyes of her sons. They huddled in the corner of the room, lost and scared and there was nothing she could do to make it all right for them. They heard the roar of the crowd gathered near the temple and all she could utter was a mumbled, "You can do this. You can get through this. Be strong and don't be afraid." Words that made her want to laugh even as she spoke, for she was drowning in her own fear.

She knew, however, that her fear couldn't hold her back. She knew that she couldn't just hide away and do nothing, so she gathered her courage and moved out into the swirling chaos. Following the crowd streaming out of the city she wound her way to the end of the road. Three crosses filled the field of vision. On the center Jesus hung— bruised and bleeding. And on his right and on his left hung two strangers. She felt a sob lodge in her throat. On his right and on his left . . . that is where she had asked to see her sons. On his right and on his left . . . this is the kingdom of love? Yet even as a wail of loss and fear rose up from deep within, Jesus' eyes met hers and a small thread of peace began weaving through her pain. In spite of the awfulness, in spite of the raging grief, she sensed that this was not the final chapter.

Three days passed. Three days of loneliness and weeping. Three days of shadows and gloom. And then, Mary came running into the heart of grief with a word so amazing that she knew it had to be true. Jesus was not dead, but alive. His kingdom was not defeated, but just beginning. On his right, on his left, beside him, behind him . . . wherever she was, wherever her sons were, they were just where they should be. And she knew. Love had won.

12

The Cowardly Lion: Peter

Matthew 4:18–22, 26:69–75, John 21:1–19

I N THE rough and tumble world of fishermen, Peter was the roughest—and not afraid of a tumble or two. Even as a youngster he showed no sign of fear, always ready to climb a little higher and jump a little farther than the other boys. He was the one in the front of the pack when trouble came, and while he never started a fight, he never, ever walked away from one. The other boys admired his gutsy approach to authority figures—local rabbis, visiting priests, Roman soldiers—none of them seemed to intimidate him in the least. His parents worried all the time, for his brashness often led to trouble. His encounters earned him many a black eye and more than his share of bruises, but nothing seemed to slow him down. He was fearless—and if he had given it thought, he would have been the first to admit it. But as a man of impulsive action rather than careful consideration, he didn't give it or anything else much thought.

Fishing was a perfect job for this man with nerves of steel, for the challenge of wind and wave invigorated him. He loved every part of the job—except net mending. His hands that could cast a net far and wide became clumsy and awkward as he tried to untangle knots and thread a needle. He had no patience with the idle chatter of his companions and sitting for more than ten minutes drove him into a restless state of toe-tapping, leg-bouncing nervousness. Maybe that is why he was the first one to notice the man moving along the shore line, a man clearly out of his element with too-clean clothing and too-smooth hands, yet who walked with the sure-footed stride of one who was familiar with the lay of the land. As the stranger neared the fishermen, Peter saw him lift his head and take a deep breath of the salty, fishy air and smile. Not worrying about the state of his robe, the man crouched down amid the slimy nets and picked up a strand in his hands. Peter watched those hands as they began weaving the frayed ends of the net, restoring its torn fragments into a seamless whole.

"What is your name?" Peter blurted out.

The man turned and spoke so quietly that Peter had to lean forward to hear. "I'm Jesus, from Nazareth. I'm looking for a few good men to come with me on a mission that will change the world. You look like just the man I need. Follow me."

Peter lifted his head and saw Jesus' eyes fixed on him. That was all it took. In a matter of seconds, Peter—brave, fearless Peter—rose to his feet, grabbed the bag containing his lunch—and began walking. Oblivious to his colleague's questions and even his father's stunned, anguished gasp, Peter moved forward with no backward look.

At first, it seemed as if this new life was made just for him. Each day with Jesus was a new adventure—for Jesus was also a man of courage. There were no obstacles too great to slow Jesus and his followers down. Illness melted away, storms ceased, food multiplied. It looked as if there was no stopping this band of believers on their way to greatness—to glory. Peter wasn't sure when things began to feel different, when he began to feel different. Maybe it was the day when Jesus began talking like a madman—talking about his death, and crosses and suffering. That sort of defeatist attitude rankled Peter. Convinced that the slightest hint of doubt could only set them on the road to failure, Peter tried to rally him with words of encouragement and set Jesus back on the path of victory; but Jesus turned on him. Jesus didn't yell, but the tone of his voice, the intensity of his eyes, the set of his chin, made it clear that Peter's advice was unnecessary, unwanted, and unacceptable. Peter's words died away and for the first time in his life he stepped back from controversy.

Or maybe it was the day in the boat. Jesus had sent them on ahead, but in the early morning, Peter saw Jesus moving across the water toward him. When Jesus called, Peter—brave fearless Peter—leapt from the boat and began walking on the water. But even as the cool water lapped against the sole of his foot, he felt a thin trickle of fear in the pit of his stomach. Walk on the water? This can't be! And even as he felt fear rising, he found himself sinking, choking as water filled his nose and his throat. It was only the strong arms of Jesus that got him out of that one. Peter didn't sleep so well after that. Each night, as the sun set, he felt his uneasiness rise and although he covered his anxiety with loud talk, he began to think more about what was happening, trying to convince himself that he could cope with trouble

When Jesus told them that they were headed to Jerusalem, the other disciples were worried. Some tried to stop Jesus, others began whispering to each other. Peter brushed away their concern. "Don't worry," he blustered. "We can handle anything. I won't start a fight, but I won't run away from one, either."

At first, he thought maybe it would all be all right. As they entered the city, the welcoming cheers lifted all their spirits. But it only took a few hours, to realize that the welcome covered a seething, angry hostility that swirled around them like a dark cloud. For the first time in his life, Peter, the brave, knew that he was truly afraid.

Usually he looked forward to the Passover meal with its familiar rituals and special food. But this year, nothing was right. Jesus seemed a bit withdrawn—sad even. James and John were bickering and Judas wouldn't meet Peter's eyes. Peter choked down as much of the food as he could manage, but before he could make his exit, Jesus began talking. Strange words that only made Peter more afraid—words about broken bodies and blood poured out. Peter wanted to scream to Jesus to stop. To be quiet. And then Jesus said something that frightened Peter more than anything had ever done before. He said, "One of you here at this table will betray me." Peter felt a cold chill move from his feet to his head. Jesus must have gotten inside his mind. Jesus knew how he doubted him. Jesus knew he wasn't brave and tough. He heard himself mumble something about never letting Jesus down. About always sticking with him. About finishing the fight. And he prayed it was true.

The rest of the evening was a blur of shadows and darkness. He remembered walking what seemed like miles to a garden where they collapsed under some olive trees. He remembered Jesus asking him to wait while he prayed. He remembered promising—but the next thing he remembered was waking up to the sound of swords clanking and Roman boots on the stones. Then Jesus was gone—dragged away into the darkness. He couldn't find any of the other disciples, and he didn't know what to do. Panic rose up in him until it burst out in one long anguished scream, and then he took off running, hoping that fatigue might banish the fear. He followed the lanterns bobbing ahead of him to the courtyard of the high priest. His breath coming in short, gasps he collapsed behind one of the large pillars. Waiting. Waiting. Finally he could stand it no longer, so, pulling his cloak around his head he inched toward the fire where some of the servants of the priest were warming their hands.

One of them turned and said to him, "I know you, don't I?"

Peter opened his mouth to say, yes, you saw me with Jesus. But the words that came out were, "I don't know what you mean."

Again, she pushed him and again he brushed her aside. But she wouldn't give up and so a third time he blurted out his denial of Jesus. And then, as a rooster crowed in the distance, he knew what he had done. He had run from the greatest fight of his life. He had backed away when Jesus needed him the most. He had let Jesus down—and tears, wrenched from his heart, filled the furrows of his face. He was afraid.

Again Peter ran. He ran for cover. He ran as far and as fast as he could, hoping to get away from the shame and the pain, refusing to watch any more of the horror. At first he nursed his wounds alone, but then Andrew found him and brought him to the room where the others were also cowering. Hoping that locked doors would keep the soldiers away from them. Hoping that locked doors would keep them from facing the demons of guilt and regret and grief. It was there that Mary found them. Early in the morning, her cries woke Peter and his old instincts kicked in. She told him that Jesus' body was gone and Peter went running. Half-hoping that Jesus was alive, and half-fearing that he was alive. For if the body had not been carried away by the Romans, if Jesus were alive, what would he have to say to Peter?

The tomb was empty. Empty. An emptiness that nurtured Peter's fear, fed his uncertainty and doubt. So Peter did the only thing he knew to do. He went fishing. He went back to the wind and waves where he felt confident and strong.

All that day and all that night he waited. Finally as the dawn rose over the water, he looked toward the shore and saw a thin wisp of smoke curling into the sky. He rubbed his eyes in disbelief. Could it be? Impossible! Maybe? It was . . . the figure by the fire was Jesus. The other disciples began rowing to shore, but Peter couldn't wait. Better to face Jesus' anger and rage sooner rather than later. So Peter jumped into the water and swam his way to . . . well, he would find out soon enough. Dripping his way across the shore, he prepared his words of apology. Yet it was Jesus who spoke first. "Peter," he said as a gentle smile crossed his face. "Peter, do you love me?"

"Oh, yes," Peter burst out. "I love you and will follow you anywhere."

"Good," Jesus said. "Feed my sheep." Then he intensi-fied his gaze. "Peter," he said, "do you love me?" "Oh, Jesus, I do," Peter choked out. "Don't doubt it. I do." "Good," Jesus said. "Take care of my lambs."

Peter sank to the ground as Jesus said yet again, "Peter, do you love me?" "Please," Peter, cried, "please believe me. I do love you." "Good," Jesus said, "Now you can go to work. Reach out to the lonely; help the wounded. Offer courage to those who are afraid."

Each word poured over Peter like a cool shower on a hot day, like soothing balm on blistered hands. Peter had allowed his fear to get in the way. He had thought that he could do anything on his own. That he could push and con-trol any situation. And he had seen how weak he really was. Three times he had allowed his weakness to separate him from Jesus. And now Jesus had turned that around. Three times Jesus had offered Peter grace and forgiveness. And now Peter knew that fear wasn't the problem. The problem came when he tried to handle that fear by himself. But with Jesus . . . well, there was nothing he could not do. Not any illness or injury, no failure or disappointment, nothing in life or in death, no guilt or grief, nothing could pull him out of Christ's love.

He looked at Jesus as if memorizing his features. He looked at the other disciples huddled around the fire. And he knew what he had to do. He knew that it was time for him to get out of the boat and to start walking. Across the water. Through the wilderness. Into the hearts of cities and towns—wherever people needed hope. Slowly Peter rose to his feet and with a smile he set off, ready to meet whatever challenge God placed before him with courage and joy.

13

Out of the Shadows: Malchus

John 18:1–11

SOMETIMES MALCHUS wondered if he had been rendered invisible. Why else could he walk through a room filled with people who looked right through him as if he didn't exist? He wanted to shout, "Look at me. My heart beats just like yours. I have two hands and two feet just like you. I'm right here. Can't you see?" But Malchus also knew what happened to slaves who drew attention to themselves. Punishment was quick and severe, and he had learned at an early age to keep a low profile. He had been a slave for so many years, that he had almost forgotten how it felt to be seen as a human being. There were times when he began to wonder if his flesh was fading away. Days when he would check the water in the barrel behind the chief priest's house to make sure a watery image looked back at him. The only time anyone, other than his fellow slaves, addressed him was when there was work to do or he had done something wrong, and as unpleasant as those encounters were at least he knew he had some substance.

Occasionally when his master Caiaphas sent him on an errand, Malchus was able to sneak in a quick conversation with others like himself. But even then, he felt like an outsider. They seemed to think that just because he was slave to the high priest—a holy man—he had an easy life. Whenever he heard that sort of grumbling, he would laugh, "You couldn't be more wrong. He's impossible to please, demanding this and that. Looking down his nose with a pious glare that shrivels even the most devoted Pharisee."

Malchus woke up every morning with a start—fear gripping him before he even put his feet on the floor. Fear of drawing the wrong sort of attention to himself. Fear of making a mistake. Fear of being late or arriving early. Fear of being in the right place at the wrong time or the wrong place at the right time. Fear of not knowing what was right and what was wrong. Fear of being ignored one more time. Fear of being noticed and getting the wrong sort of attention. Every step he took, every word he uttered was thought about and anguished over. Convinced that his life was as bad as it could be, he was horrified to discover that things only got worse after the Galilean known as Jesus came to town. For weeks Caiaphas and his cohorts were nervous and on edge—reacting harshly to the slightest error in judgment. Malchus heard whispered rumors of this man who dared to flout the religious rules of purity and order. Angry discussions centered on this itinerant rabbi who consorted with sinners and talked about loving enemies. Malchus couldn't help but think that a little invisibility might do Jesus of Nazareth some good, but instead of keeping a low profile, this Jesus seemed intent on being noticed—parading through the streets of Jerusalem on a donkey like some sort of king, attacking the money changers in the temple. When Malchus heard about the coins rolling everywhere and the birds swooping through the crowds, he wanted to laugh out loud. Wisely, however, when Caiaphas walked through the room with bird droppings dotting his robe, he controlled his smile.

It was later that night that Malchus made the mistake of walking into a room without knocking. Caiaphas turned with a look that froze Malchus in place and the thin man Caiaphas was addressing as Judas jumped as if he had touched a hot stove. Malchus backed out as quickly as he could and wisely made himself scarce for the next several hours. Later that evening, Caiaphas burst into the slave quarters. "Get up and get dressed," he barked. "Go on with the Temple police and do whatever they tell you." The tone of his voice and the intensity etched into his face caused the slaves to scramble and in seconds they were out the door. The captain of the guard grabbed Malchus by the shoulder, threw him into one of the lines, and thrust a club into his hands. And before Malchus could blink they were headed through the gates of the city, across the Kidron valley, and up a hill to a garden filled with olive trees.

Later, when he thought about that night, the thing he remembered most of all was the darkness. It wasn't the pitch darkness of a moonless night, but a darkness that was alive with undercurrents of fear, alive with lurking monsters. Soon the silence of the garden was shattered with pounding feet and calling voices, the clanging of swords and armor, and a rustling in the air—a sound that sent shivers through Malchus despite the heat. A sound of flapping wings and rustling leaves. Fear began to rise up in him until he felt as if he would drown in the stinking fetid torrent. Then as he entered into the center of the garden, the smoking torches revealed a few men stumbling to their feet, rubbing their eyes, easing the stiffness from their bones. One man, however stood out from the rest—his clothes crumpled and as wet as if he had been running in the heat of the day. This man was wide awake and as he moved out of the shadows toward them, Malchus heard the man next to him chuckle, "Look at that Jesus. He doesn't look like much of a king to me." As Malchus continued to watch, he saw the thin man he had last seen in Caiaphas' study moving slowly toward Jesus until they stood toe to toe. As he leaned forward to kiss Jesus on the cheek, he whispered something that Malchus couldn't make out. In that instant Malchus felt a sadness wash over him. There was something so awful and painful about what he was witnessing that he could hardly stand erect. Maybe it was the way Jesus' eyes darkened with pain and grief. Maybe it was the way Jesus body seemed to sag as if a great load had been dropped on his shoulders. Maybe it was the way the thin man drew back as if he had been stabbed through the heart. Maybe it was the silence—no more wind. No bird calls. No crickets. As if all creation were holding its breath. Then Jesus blinked as if to clear his mind. He straightened his back, and the air exploded. Voices shouting orders. Screams of fear. People running and bumping into each other. Suddenly a huge shape hurtled past Jesus bellowing and slashing the air with a short sword.

At first Malchus thought a stinging insect had attacked his ear, but a few seconds later pain exploded and as he pulled his hand from his head it was wet with blood. And he screamed. All his pain, his humiliation, all the loss and grief and disappointment of his life were in that scream. Even as he opened his mouth to scream again, he felt a hand on his head and a warmth began to work its way into the bleeding hole. He opened his eyes and there was Jesus with eyes so filled with love and understanding, that Malchus' scream died away. Jesus looked at him and into him and through him and Malchus felt a healing energy moving into all the broken and beaten down places in his spirit.

Ever since he was a young boy and carried off into slavery, Malchus had been told that he was nobody. He was worthless. And now this Jesus reached out to him— to Malchus, an unimportant slave—and he was made new. For as long as he could remember Malchus had dealt with his fear and pain by pushing them so deep inside that he could almost forget that they were there. But now it was as if someone had reached into his heart and brought all the darkness, all the bitter longing, all the unshed tears, all the anguished loneliness to the surface where it was cut away. Malchus knew that Jesus had healed more than his ear. Jesus had touched him and Malchus was free.

14

Pax Romana: Pilate

Matthew 27:11–26

Pilate was tired. Tired of working hard and watching others get promoted. Tired of constantly looking over his shoulder for backstabbing friends. Tired of living by principles of justice and honor only to watch the unprincipled climb to positions of authority. All he had ever wanted was to have his name connected with the glory of Rome, to be listed among the great and powerful in the empire, to accomplish great things for Rome so that in the years to come poets would write of his life. He had spent all his adult life getting to know the right people; carefully making his way through the often-tricky political landscape that was Rome. He studied the influential men around him and learned quickly to keep his opinions to himself, cultivating the ability to speak only what others wanted to hear. He gave gifts when they were needed, did favors when asked, and carefully calculated what to do to position himself for a prestigious appointment from Caesar.

And look where it got him. Judea?! Nobody wanted this volatile, backwater province. But, it was always dangerous to say no to Caesar, so Pilate packed his bags and moved south. As he looked back through the years, he recognized that it was that move that transformed worry into fear . . . a gut wrenching, gnawing dread that never left him. Judea was a no-win situation. Trying to keep the peace that Rome required in the midst of the stubborn worshippers of Yahweh had broken better men than he. How could you intimidate a people who refused to acknowledge any authority other than that of their strange, demanding God?

Pilate knew, however, that he had no real choice and, during the day at least, he attempted to manage the people so that trouble did not boil over. Pilate was tired of stress and strain. Tired of stubborn Jews and short-tempered Roman soldiers. Tired of keeping peace in the midst of simmering anger and resentment.

Eventually he became used to the heat, the looks of hate, and the unreasonable attitude of the people, but he never got used to springtime. Most people welcomed the warm breezes and sweet-smelling flowers. Children darted through the greening grass, young men whistled as they worked and old men smiled more often, But as Pilate listened to the birds singing and caught the whiff of lilacs, his stomach knotted and his shoulders tensed. For him, spring meant only one thing—Passover. Passover—when religiously inspired crowds packed the narrow streets and alleys of Jerusalem. Passover—when emotions ran high and Jewish zealots stretched their muscles. One never knew what trouble might rise up. The prudent action was to situate himself so that he could keep track of what was going on, and that meant leaving the relative comfort of his court in Caesarea for the uncertain tension of Jerusalem.

He never knew a good springtime, but there was one particular Passover that haunted him forever. That year the city pulsed with dis-ease. Tensions simmered under the surface of every conversation, every business transaction. Extra men patrolled the streets, and the jails were full. Pilate increased his guard and even carried a sword whenever he left his palace. One day he attempted to check out a suspected terrorist threat at the temple. He could hear angry screams while he was still blocks away. A group of temple staff almost ran him down. He grabbed one of them by the back of his robe.

"What is going on?" Pilate demanded.

The man's anger overcame his fear and he snapped back, "A lot of good you Romans are? Where is your famous peace? That fool burst into our temple market and went mad. He turned the tables over and all my livestock are running somewhere in the city. That is they are running around if the thieving pilgrims haven't already eaten them. What are you going to do about it?"

Before Pilate could respond, the man jerked himself away with such energy that Pilate was left holding a scrap of his robe. Pilate's stomach began to churn. Another incident like this and he would have no choice but to occupy the temple—and that would not happen without bloodshed— much bloodshed. He prayed to every god that he could think of to keep the people from inciting any action that might disturb the peace, and for awhile thought maybe he would make it until the end of the holiday when the crowds had left. But that Friday he was jolted out of a deep, dreamless sleep by what sounded at first like a swarm of buzzing bees. He tried to block out the sound, but as the intensity and fervor grew, Pilate rose from his bed. Splashing some water on his face and wrapping the sheet from his bed around him, he peered out the window. He could feel the pressure in his chest tighten as he saw dozens of angry men filling the courtyard. Beads of sweat popped out on his head as he recognized a few of them as the leaders of the Temple. Whatever it was that brought Jews to the Roman governor, it must be trouble. Pilate uttered a string of curses, causing the servant waiting to dress him to cringe and sidle out of the room as quickly as possible.

As Pilate stalked out onto the portico, his eyes went at once to a figure standing with hands bound and head held high. "Who is this man and why are you bothering me with your problems?" Pilate thundered. Pilate tried to listen to the temple representative's explanation, but it made no sense. The priest muttered some nonsense about this man claiming to be a king. It was ridiculous. There was nothing regal about this poor, beaten, exhausted-looking human being. But, sensing the crowd's razor-sharp anger, Pilate decided to go along with the charade.

"Is that true?" he asked. "Are you the king of the Jews?"

He had to strain to hear the answer over the roar of the crowd. "You say so," the man replied, looking at Pilate with a look of such pity and love that Pilate's breath caught in his throat. "The man must be delusional," Pilate muttered to himself. "He may be crazy, but he is no threat to Rome."

Pilate tried everything. He sent him to Herod. He re-examined him. Then, to make a bad situation worse, his wife appeared. Clutching his sleeve, she whispered, "Don't get involved in this. I dreamed about this very man last night and you should have nothing to do with him."

Her terror was contagious. Pilate longed to scream and scream until everyone vanished, but what could he do? All he could hear were cries of, "Crucify him! Crucify him!" The noise was driving him mad. But that wasn't as bad as the silence of this man they called Jesus. Caught between the screams and the silence, between rage and calm, Pilate was trapped. And so, for the good of Rome, for the good of the empire, for his own good, he nodded toward the soldiers to take him away to the place of execution. That seemed to make the crowds happy, but just in case . . . just to cover his bets . . . wanting to absolve himself of any guilt . . . Pilate dipped his hands in a nearby basin of water. He hoped to wash himself clean of any wrongdoing he might have done. But as he dipped his hands in the cool water, fear sank its claws into his heart and began shredding his heart. It didn't kill him, although many a sleepless night he wished it had. It just coiled up inside of him, tainting every breath with anguished regret, poisoning every relationship with distrust, eating away at joy. Fear destroyed him long before he took his final breath. Every year, when the spring breezes blew, he longed to rewind the clock, to relive that moment, to have the courage to say this man is innocent. To have the courage to say love is stronger than hate. What if? What if he had aligned himself with justice and truth? What if he had immersed himself in the goodness of the one called Jesus?

What if he had acted out of integrity? What if . . .

15

Amazing Grace: Mary Magdalene

John 20:1–18

SOMETIMES THE darkness threatened to swallow her alive. Other days, wave after wave of frantic energy surged beneath her skin until she thought she would explode. One day, fatigue leached the colors from sky and trees, leaving her collapsed in a dusty gray world. The next day, light flashed and burned, until her head pounded and her eyes ached. One moment she would be crouched in the shadows hoping to fade away to nothing and then the next she would be running and laughing and talking a mile a minute—even if there was no one there to listen. And there often wasn't, for no one wanted to get too close to Crazy Mary.

In her brief lucid moments, she longed for the sort of anonymity one might find in Jerusalem's shadowy alleys and byways. But she lived in Magdala, the sort of place where everybody knew your name . . . and every detail of your past and present. Like many villages, it was small enough that sometimes it seemed as if people knew more about their neighbors than their neighbors knew about themselves. And the residents of Magdala knew that Mary was trouble. Her reputation for destructive and inappropriate behavior had even spread into neighboring villages where young girls were warned, "Behave yourself or you'll turn out like Mary Magdalene."

It hadn't always been like that. Once Mary laughed and played like any other girl. She shared whispered dreams and secrets with her friends. But as she entered her teens, the laughter took on a disturbing edge. Her mood shifted so quickly and dramatically that her friends began avoiding her. Her mother tried to restrain her, with moderate success. It was her mother's death from a sudden illness that pushed Mary over the edge. With no one to calm her frantic activity or coax her from the fog of depression, any hope of stability dissipated. Years went by. Years of scornful glances and muttered insults.

Mary's mantra became "I don't care what you think. I only care what I think." She shrieked it at the women gathering at the well, laughing as their faces tightened with disapproval. She whispered it as she passed groups of men working in the fields. She chanted it whenever she saw children at play, enjoying the resulting fear and confusion. But the truth was . . . she did care. Mary's chaotic confusion didn't keep her from knowing how bizarre she was. She hated the whispers and the way the women pulled their children close when she drew near. Each morning she opened her eyes and prayed that things would be different, that the voices in her head would be silent, that her neighbors wouldn't draw away when she drew near. But even before her sleeping pallet was rolled up, she began spiraling out of control. One day bled into another, a whirlwind of madness.

Then one day, in one moment, a moment as brief as that between one breath and another, it all changed. That day the battle between depression and hysterical euphoria was fierce. People were talking about a new rabbi from Galilee, but she couldn't stop her dance of madness long enough to pay attention. She almost missed him. But as she whirled in her dance of madness, there he was bathed in the sunlight. Why this man captured her attention puzzled her, for there was nothing particularly striking about him. And yet . . . there was something. Gathering her courage, she inched her way toward him—ignoring the hands reaching out to pull her back. Nearing him, she whispered, "I care what you think. I care what you think." He turned to look at her and as he did Mary felt a blessed emptiness unfolding deep inside—a vast space freed of all the rage and sadness that had gripped her for so long. And then, before she could blink, a gentle joy wrapped itself around her, a joy that changed everything. Instead of a jumble of voices she heard birds chirping and babies giggling. Instead of the threatening darkness, she saw clouds dancing across the blue sky and green bushes dotted with pink azaleas. Her breathing slowed and with a deep sigh of contentment she smiled.

The next few weeks brought Mary a peace unlike anything she had ever known. Instead of smothering in gray clouds of misery and confusion, she took deep breaths of clean air, air alive with power and promise. Everyone noticed, and they weren't necessarily happy. They expected Crazy Mary to be, well . . . crazy. Her calm demeanor puzzled them. Village leaders regarded her with suspicious caution. Conversations died away as she approached. Children darted for home as she neared. But instead of retaliating with angry tirades, Mary just smiled and waited, and as the days and weeks passed, things began to change. People began to look her in the eye, to offer a quick, shy smile, to mumble a casual good morning.

And she wasn't just finding acceptance in Magdala. Even though Jesus' followers acted as if she weren't there, brushing off her questions and concerns as if she were invisible, Jesus' patient friendship breathed new life into her spirit. Rooted and grounded in love, Mary thrived. But she was careful not to wander too far from Jesus. Listening to his stories, watching him move among the crowds, gave her meaning and purpose. And the closer she drew to Jesus, the closer she drew to the others until one day she looked around and realized that she was part of a fellowship of caring and concern that healed any remaining soreness in her soul. And so the days passed in a rhythm of learning and helping, listening and talking, working and resting.

She didn't think twice when Jesus said it was time to move on. She packed up her few belongings and was on the way in a matter of moments. Life on the road wasn't always comfortable. Sometimes they were wined and dined as if they were royalty. Other times, they slept on the hard ground after a skimpy supper. But no matter how rough the journey, Mary found joy just by being in Jesus' presence.

She also found a purpose for her life. When they entered a new town, Mary began standing at the back of the gathered crowd. She looked for the woman or child who stood in the shadows, hesitant to move forward. She watched for the person who pulled back from the rest of those gathered. When she found someone like that, she would quietly move to stand beside them. Engaging them in conversation, she offered the loving mercy she herself had received, trying to let them know that they weren't alone. Sometimes it didn't seem to make a difference—the person would dart away or turn away. But most of the time, the eagerness with which her friendship was received gave her the courage to keep trying.

She would gladly have spent the rest of her life like this, but all too soon, an uneasiness worked its way into her heart. Jesus' speech took on an urgency that was worrisome. He began speaking in terrifying riddles—talking about crosses and death in ways that just didn't make sense. Late at night those closest to him whispered to each other their concern and their fear. Some even threatened to head back home if he didn't change his tune. Others thought that he was only waiting for the right moment to unleash his power . . . and they wanted to be present when that happened. Mary didn't know what to think; so she just listened to them . . . and to Jesus . . . storing each word he spoke in her heart. Late at night lying under the star-spangled sky, she would play these words over and over in her mind, trying to make sense of them.

Her concern only deepened as she realized that the road they were on was leading inexorably to Jerusalem. One day she gathered up all her courage and blurted out her fear and doubt to Jesus. "Please," she begged. "Don't go there. There are those there who love you, but even more are jealous of you and will go to any lengths to keep you from increasing your power. They hate you; don't you know that?

Look at us—we'll be pitiful bodyguards. I couldn't bear it if anything happened to you."

Jesus looked at her then—a look of such love and sadness that the words caught in her throat. "Mary," he said. "Mary, this is the road of love."

That was the last chance they had for private conversation. A few days later they entered the city, and events began spinning faster than she could keep up with. Reality became so confusing and horrifying that she almost wished she could retreat into her former madness, and forget it all. Each day brought a new tension, a new fear. Hostile religious leaders, angry Roman officials—each encounter led Jesus closer to his doom.

Mary watched in disbelief as Jesus' followers melted away. She could understand the reaction of the casual bystanders, but Peter and Thomas, Judas and John? She began to be very afraid. For if those strong men who had been through so much with Jesus and knew him so well crumbled, what would happen to her?

Even the Passover meal—that great celebration of God's presence—took on shadowy overtones. No one ate much, especially when Jesus started talking about bodies being broken and blood being poured out. She was relieved when Jesus and the men left for a time of prayer. She normally didn't enjoy cleaning up after a meal, but that night it was a relief to have something to do—anything to keep her from thinking. However, before she was finished a couple of the disciples burst through the door.

"They've got him," one of them gasped.

The blood drained from her head and the pounding of her heart drowned out the rest of what they said. All she knew was that the one she loved more than life itself was in trouble. Reeling from the shock, she headed for the door, but one of the disciples grabbed her and thrust her back into the room.

"Don't be a fool," he shouted. "There's nothing you can do. There's nothing any of us can do. It's all over."

Mary huddled in the corner, too distraught to even cry. But, as the sun began to rise, she knew that there was something she could do. She could be there. If Jesus was suffering, she could at least let him know he was not alone. She could stand with him so that in the midst of hate and anger, he would also see the look of love. So that, even if the worst happened, at the end he would know that he was not alone.

That terrible Friday she watched as Jesus was led through the streets and alleys—his poor broken, bruised, bleeding body an object of ridicule. She wanted to run and hide, but she stood her ground. Even as she heard nails pounded into soft flesh, she focused her eyes on him, not flinching from the horror, but looking and loving with all her strength. She waited and waited under a brutally hot sun, listening to Jesus' raspy breaths—and then she heard nothing except her own scream of grief.

Mary never knew how she got back to the room where the others were hiding. All she wanted to do was go to sleep and never wake up again. Traumatized by all she had seen and heard, she curled up in a corner, turned her head to the wall, and waited. She might have lain there forever, but finally she felt a hand on her shoulder. She turned and looked into Peter's face—a face so contorted by grief and shame that her own grief receded for a moment. "Mary," he choked. "Mary, they say you were there at the end. Tell me, please."

What did he want? Did he want all the brutal details? If he cared so much, why hadn't he been there? She opened her mouth to pour out her anger and scorn, but as she looked into his wounded eyes, she saw the heartbreak and loneliness of one standing on the edge of life and so she simply said, "His last words were, 'Father, forgive them.'"

Then Peter's tears mingled with her own, and as they wept some of her sorrow washed away. For three days they shared memories, they cried, they clung to one another—Peter and Mary, James and John, and the others. Grateful as she was to have others to weep with, as the Sabbath ended, she knew what she had to do. And she knew she needed to be alone.

While it was still dark, in the early morning mists, Mary slipped out of the house and moved quietly through Jerusalem. Wanting one last moment with Jesus to bathe his broken body and say goodbye, she came to the tomb. Peering through the darkness she was horrified to see only emptiness—no body, nothing. As fast as she could she ran back to the others. Heading straight for Peter she gasped out, "He's gone. They've taken him. Do something." Peter and one other—in the confusion she wasn't sure which one—didn't wait for Mary to gather herself together, but took off running through the tangled streets and alleys. When she finally caught up with them, they were already walking out of the tomb, shaking their heads in dismay. It hit her like a hammer blow to the heart. He was gone. The icy breath of fear covered Mary and all she could do was weep. Without him . . . what would become of her? The ground shifted under her feet, and she looked into that old, familiar abyss of pain. She could already hear the whispers, "She's back. Crazy Mary is back." She wanted to scream, but all that came out was a dull groan.

Then the leaves rustled behind her and she twirled around to see a man. "You must be the caretaker," she gasped. "Please, you have to tell me. Where is the body?"

"Mary," he said.

One word, that's all she heard. And with that word she is bathed in warmth and joy. All the pieces fall into place. His life, her life, all the tangled threads of sin and grace, hope and despair, longing and peace. Mary knew. Even when the worst that can happen happens . . . it is not the end. Nothing, not even death, is strong enough to pull apart that which is connected by grace. And that is enough. Enough light to banish the darkness. Enough mercy to erase all guilt. Enough love to cast out fear.

16

Scales of Love: Ananias

Acts 9:1–19

E VEN BEFORE the doctor left the room, word began to spread. Followers of the Way began to whisper to one another as they passed through the streets of Damascus, "He's dying. Ananias is dying." As the sun shifted below the rooftops, they began to gather, quietly gliding through the streets and alleys to the place of meeting. The worship leader for the week lit the candles and as he turned to face his friends, he said. "Our brother Ananias will soon be with the Lord and for him we are glad. But our hearts are heavy, for the light of his faith has helped to illuminate our path for many years and we will miss him."

As the service progressed, a small group of children began fidgeting and whispering. One of the women eased her way into their midst, and as she did one of the young girls tugged on her skirt. "Judith," she whispered, "who is Ananias?" Judith placed her finger to her lips and whispered, "I'll tell you later."

The children quieted, but Judith's thoughts began swirling. Who is Ananias? The children may be too young to remember him, but she could still see the young man striding through the streets, head craning forward as if he couldn't wait to see what was around the bend. And she could almost hear him whistling—for his simple tunes served as the call to worship in the early years. Who is Ananias? Maybe it wasn't too late for these children to hear his story.

And so it was that after worship, Judith and the children made their way to a small room in a building tucked away behind the marketplace. The sunlight was fading, but a flickering candle lit up the shape of a man stretched out on a pallet in the corner under the window. At first, the adults crammed into the narrow space tried to send them away, but then a husky voice muttered, "Let them in. They want to see me and I need to look at the future."

"We are praying for you," Judith began. "May God grant you peace. If you have the strength, these children would like to hear your story. Could you talk with them?"

Ananias raised his hand and beckoned them closer. "Sit here," he said, "close to me so you can hear. Listen and remember."

I'm never sure how to explain what happened to me. I often envied those who could describe when and where they met the power and grace of God. It wasn't that clear-cut for me. I don't even remember when it was that I first heard about the events in Jerusalem. All I know is that one year those who had gone to Jerusalem to celebrate the great festival of Pentecost returned with strange stories of a Galilean carpenter-turned-teacher who dared to challenge the powers of Rome itself. Some even claimed to have met people who had seen this Jesus after he had been killed and buried. There were whispers of miraculous healings, of nobodies being welcomed as somebodies, of a dead man being raised to life. As I heard their stories—as I saw joy and energy radiating from those who told them—I began to be more and more curious. I asked questions. I began to spend more time with the men and women who followed this Way, and gradually I knew that this Jesus of Nazareth offered me something I couldn't find anywhere else, and so I was baptized.

The new life Christ promised wasn't easy. Some of my family and a lot of my friends thought I had lost my mind. But a new community of believers welcomed me and offered encouragement and support. We gathered weekly for worship and to share what we had—and some weeks that was very little. A couple members of our group were well off, but most of us barely made ends meet. But as we pooled our resources, we not only survived but were able to help others in need. This community became my family— together we struggled to understand what this new way of life was all about. We prayed together and ate together and worshipped together and studied together and worked together. And soon we suffered together. I guess anything new arouses suspicion and we were certainly something new. Jew and Gentile, slave and free, men and women spending time together shocked and horrified those who sought racial and religious purity. Rome resented our unwillingness to put them first in our hearts and saw our devotion to God as unpatriotic and they turned on us with angry venom.

Rome's rage, however, was nothing compared to the bitter rage of the Temple authorities who saw us as heretics and turncoats. Word came to us from Jerusalem and other parts of Israel of terrible consequences to the faithful there—of men and women, even children, being dragged off to prison and worse. As these storm clouds moved our way from all directions, we began watching our words carefully, finding out-of-the-way places to gather, walking a tightrope of faith across a chasm of fear.

One thing we could do was pray and I did that often—praying that God would keep me safe. Praying that God would keep me faithful if the worst happened. Praying that God would cast those who persecuted us into the prisons with which they threatened us. Then one day as I was in prayer, the name Saul entered my mind. Now, that wasn't too surprising, for we had been talking about Saul a great deal. Men and women who had turned to Christ were being arrested, tortured, some even killed. And it was fire-breathing Saul who was leading the persecution. At first we thought that we were so far from Jerusalem, the religious leaders would leave us alone. But we didn't count on Saul's zealous determination. One day we heard that he was on his way with orders from the high priest to find and "handle" us.

I know I should have been strong and fearless, but I was afraid. It is easy to be courageous if you aren't put to the test, but in the face of ridicule, humiliation, pain . . . did I have the faith I needed? That's why I was praying. I didn't want to let my brothers and sisters down. I didn't want to let Jesus down. But I was scared. So Saul was the focus of my praying. I prayed that God would get him, that God would get rid of him, that God would keep him away from us.

Even as I was saying these words, I felt a stirring deep within.

"Ananias, I need you."

"Lord, is it you? I'll do whatever you ask," I said.

"Go to Straight Street."

"Right away!"

"There you'll find a man who needs you. One who needs someone with hands of grace. One who needs to hear your song of healing mercy."

"I'm on my way."

"A man named Saul."

"Saul?! Wait a minute. There must be a mistake. In the first place, I don't know enough to teach anyone anything. In the second place, I'll look silly if I say I'm going to heal him and then nothing happens. In the third place, what will the others think if they know I've been talking to the enemy? In the fourth place . . . well, this is Saul! Don't you know he has orders to arrest us? I don't want anything to do with him. Why should I set myself up for rejection and suffering? I'm not gifted with words. Don't you know all that? You still want me to go?"

But silence was the only reply. I waited for new orders. Nothing. I tried to distract myself with busyness. I tried to shut down my mind—to forget the last few moments, but nothing worked. All I could hear were echoes of "Go to Straight Street." So, finally, I went to Straight Street, hoping that when I got there I wouldn't be able to find the man. But as I turned onto the street, I saw a few men with the dusty look of travelers on a long journey gathered outside a simple structure and I knew I had reached my destination. I stopped outside the building and tried again.

"You don't really want me to go in, do you?" I muttered. Again, there was no reply. So I took a deep breath and went up the steps and there, sitting in a small room, was . . . Saul. I had pictured him as big and fierce, but what I saw was a frail-looking man huddled in the shadows. He lifted his head as I entered, and I saw that his eyes were covered with blistery scales as if he had been badly burned.

"Are you Ananias," he asked?

My breath caught in my throat. He couldn't see me. He couldn't know me or anything about me. Yet he knew my name. A wave of emotion—fear, hope, joy, anger, I'm not sure what—began deep inside me and I opened my mouth. I was more surprised than anyone to hear what come out. "Brother Saul", I said. Brother? Did I really say brother? This man who had wreaked havoc among Christians wherever he went, this man who was in Damascus to continue his vendetta—I called this man brother?

And then I noticed his hands. They were trembling. And as I looked more closely, I saw his fear, his uncertainty, his longing. "Brother Saul," I repeated. This time I reached out my hand and touched him. I don't remember exactly what I said, but as we stood there, his trembling eased. He blinked and I watched as his eyes began to focus. A grin stretched across his face and as he placed his hands on my shoulders, I knew that through the loving embrace of Christ we were truly brothers. The scales fell off our eyes that day. Saul saw a new way of living—a way of grace. And I saw, beneath the layers of his past, a man longing for love. I saw a friend.

Ananias's voice died away and a hush feel over the room. Then, even more quietly than before, he said, "My story is not about me. It isn't about Saul whom you now know as Paul. My story is about Jesus. Jesus loves you. Jesus loves each one of us, not because we are perfect, but because he sees someone worth loving. I didn't change the world in big and dramatic ways as Saul did, but I carried God's love with me everywhere I went. I didn't change the world, but I did what I could where I could, and trusted God to do the rest."

This time he closed his eyes and silence filled the room, a silence broken by the rustle of a little girl's skirt as she stood and moved to the bed. She looked closely at the man lying there and then very gently patted his hand with her own.